Freud on Freud

He put himself into psychoanalysis, in the role of both analyst and analysand. It sounds bizarre. But for one thing, there was no other psychoanalyst—Freud was it. And so far, his theories were primarily a result of treating women with hysteria. He felt that, to be universal, the principles of psychoanalysis would also have to include the male mind—a relatively normal one, namely his own. Only in this way would psychoanalysis develop into a complete theory of the mind.

Ever since he had tested cocaine on himself, Freud had always considered his own mind and body suitable for science experiments. Now he spent part of each day on the couch, examining his own childhood and events that shaped him, analyzing his own dreams and memories. "The chief patient I am preoccupied with is myself" and "my little hysteria," he wrote. Into middle age he was still plagued with depression and irritability, dizzy spells, feelings of worthlessness. He was attempting to take a giant step toward self-understanding.

But Freud himself wondered if he was doing the right thing—his self-analysis was both the first and the last in the history of psychoanalysis.

SIGMUND FREUD

KATHLEEN KRULL
ILLUSTRATED BY BORIS KULIKOV

PUFFIN BOOKS
An Imprint of Penguin Group (USA)

PUFFIN BOOKS
Published by the Penguin Group
Penguin Group (USA) LLC
375 Hudson Street
New York, New York 10014

USA * Canada * UK * Ireland * Australia
New Zealand * India * South Africa * China

penguin.com
A Penguin Random House Company

First published in the United States of America by Viking,
a division of Penguin Young Readers Group, 2006
Published by Puffin Books, a division of Penguin Young Readers Group, 2009

LIBRARY OF CONGRESS CATALOGING-IN-PUBLICATION DATA IS AVAILABLE
ISBN: 978-0-670-05892-1 (hc)

Puffin Books ISBN 978-0-14-241266-4

Designed by Jim Hoover

Printed in the United States of America

3 5 7 9 10 8 6 4 2

Welcome to Ethan Brewer, May 9, 2006
— K. K.

Acknowledgments
For help with research, the author thanks
Dr. Lawrence M. Principe, Stanley Bone, M.D.

Special thanks to Susan Cohen (Agenting Goddess),
Patricia Daniels, Sheila Cole, Janet Pascal,
Paul Brewer, Melanie Brewer,
Cindy Clevenger and the Rabbits,
and most of all, Jane O'Connor.

CONTENTS

INTRODUCTION

"If I have seen further [than other people]
it is by standing upon the shoulders of giants."

—Isaac Newton, 1675

*T*HE BRAIN HAS NOT always gotten respect.

When turning a corpse into a mummy, the ancient Egyptians used a small hook to scrape brain matter out through the nostrils. Then they threw it away. After all, the brain did so little—everyone knew that intelligence and emotions arose from the heart, which *was* carefully preserved.

Ancient Babylonians revered the liver as the true source of thought and emotion.

The great thinkers of ancient Greece were divided. Some, including Plato, concluded from early anatomical studies that the brain was the center of intelligence. However, Aristotle, that powerhouse born in 384 B.C., insisted the center of thought was in the center of the body: the heart. The brain was merely a sort of air conditioner, cooling off the body from the heat the heart made with all that thinking and feeling.

Galen, the famous physician from the second century A.D., knew the mind resided in the brain, yet his approach to treating a mentally disturbed patient was way off the mark. Galen believed that four humors, or fluids, generated by the brain—blood, phlegm, yellow bile, and black bile—determined not only physical but mental health. An excess of yellow bile caused ill temper, for example; an excess of black bile caused melancholy or depression. Diagnosis was a matter of examining urine, and "cures" were often a matter of bloodletting and vomiting to rid the body of that excess bile. Galen's four-humor theory dominated medical thought for more than a thousand years.

By the Middle Ages, surgeons—often the local barbers—were claiming that a "stone of madness" lodged in the head caused strange behavior. They would dig out bits of brain and a person could be "cured." For a fee.

Even Leonardo da Vinci, Renaissance wonderboy

and ahead of his time in so many ways, stuck to a prejudice about mental illness that was common in his day—a person's face reflected what was going on inside, for good or ill. An ugly, deformed face was the outward reflection of a twisted, sick personality.

And well into the 1700s, peasant folk commonly believed that mental illness was either punishment for sin or the work of the devil. Or a character weakness—depressed people were blamed for lacking self-control. Physicians still searched for medical causes of dementia, attributing it to bad blood, bad air, even bad food, and attempted to treat it with medicines including some made from highly poisonous plants like hellebore. The main "treatment" was to hide people with problems away and shut them up. If they weren't too troublesome you could lock up your mad uncle in the attic, or put your crazy sister out in the barn. For the uncontrollable, special hospitals kept them away from society—asylums that were more like jails.

Then came the Scientific Revolution, fully flowering in the work Isaac Newton began in the mid-1600s. The scientific method is about measuring, quantifying, observing the physical world, and testing those observations. Scientists made triumphant discoveries in areas where things can be seen—physics and chemistry, astronomy and biology. Through autopsy work in the 1600s, Thomas Willis, a British doctor, revealed that the brain was the center of both thought *and* sensation—it was a complexly structured organ, command central of the entire nervous system.

The brain—scientists began to understand exactly how essential it was to life. By the 1880s, the field of psychiatry, the medical treatment of diseases of the mind, had been born. One of its first books was by the German doctor Theodor Meynert, who specialized in the anatomy and function of the brain. Meynert was a "psychiatrist," a word just coming into use, replacing "alienist" (the patients were the "aliens," locked away in asylums, mentally alienated from real life).

So science, it appeared, could be applied to human behavior. Scientists struggled with such questions as: Why do humans act the way they do? What does the brain control? What is normal and what is abnormal behavior? Could science be used to help troubled people? Where do our bodies end and our minds begin? What is the "mind," anyway? Is it solely the turf of poets and philosophers? Or can scientists claim it as their territory as well?

Scientists started talking about the brain in two ways—as an anatomical entity and as an emotional mind. One is a physical organ that governs the nervous system, with different parts that control specific functions like speech and memory and the five senses—the neurological brain. The other is something we can't see, a mind that decides what those memories mean and how they affect us—the emotional brain.

Into the late 1800s, psychiatry flourished, but by focusing on anatomy—what the physical organ of the brain did. Early psychiatrists treating diseases of the nervous system saw mental illness as the brain being out of whack. They searched for physical reasons for brain disorders—lesions in the brain, perhaps. "The modern science of psychology," wrote American doctor William Hammond in 1876, "is neither more or less than *the science of mind considered as a physical function*."

There were some quirky detours taken while investigating the brain. Two doctors from Vienna—Franz Joseph Gall and Johann Spurzheim—promoted a popular pseudoscience called phrenology. They believed that the brain had some thirty or more separate organs, each of which controlled a different personality trait such as intelligence or criminal tendencies. Phrenologists believed that bumps on a person's skull corresponded to various organs and dictated a person's character. They would visit asylums and "prove" how the shape of the patients' heads matched their illness. Phrenologists also prized owning the skulls of geniuses. Mozart's was the trophy of one collection.

Consideration of the emotional mind, the thing that can't be seen, lagged behind the study of the physical aspects of the mind. By the nineteenth century, treatment of the emotionally disturbed may have become more humane at least, yet it remained largely ineffective. Rest cures, for example, helped give patients peace and quiet, but didn't treat the underlying causes of the sickness. No one thought of listening to patients, trying to figure out what ailed them. They spouted nonsense, so paying attention would just make them worse.

Meanwhile, as the twentieth century approached, another doctor from Vienna sat in a quiet room with troubled patients lying on a very important couch. Chain-smoking cigars, he listened and kept on listening. His faithful dog napped at his feet, trained to recognize when a patient's hour was up. Furiously the doctor would write up case studies that read like mystery stories.

He pioneered a treatment called talk therapy, based on the theory that unconscious fears can make people sick. Uncovering those fears would help banish the illness.

His name may ring a bell—Sigmund Freud.

Freud didn't answer all the questions about the emotional brain. And often the answers he did come up with were wrong. But he was among the first doctors to believe that psychology was actually a branch of science. Freud certainly didn't discount the physical brain, but he primarily dealt with emotions, through his talk therapy, or psychoanalysis. Freud theorized that the emotional mind could make the physical body ill, and that's what he wanted to treat—the memories, emotions, dreams.

"We have the means to cure what you are suffering from," he told the "Wolf Man," one of his famous patients. "Up to now, you have been looking for the causes of your illness in the chamber pot." No more looking at urine, as Galen would have, nor bumps on the skull and other notions from centuries past.

Today, because of Freud's work, we take it for

granted that there are sometimes hidden motives for what we do. We understand that childhood experiences mold our later life, that dreams may have important meaning, and that private fears may loosen their grip if discussed openly.

According to the mighty Newton, scientists make their discoveries by standing on the shoulders of those who came before them. Science is incremental, step by step, with no discovery made in a vacuum, no "Eureka!" moments. So whose shoulders did Freud stand on?

Exceptionally well-read, Freud had many mentors—one of them was Theodor Meynert—and he owed a complicated debt to the science of his day, starting with his idol Charles Darwin's revolutionary theory of evolution. But in inventing a system and vocabulary for studying the emotional brain—used for generations after him—he largely worked alone. Many (including Freud himself at times) questioned whether he was a true scientist—his work didn't have some of the hallmarks of the scientific method, like experiments with results that could be duplicated. He felt jealous of people in sciences like physics who could present proof for their theories—he admitted he didn't have it (yet).

Freud was like an explorer, hacking through a thorny jungle all alone. "No wonder that my path is not a very broad one, and that I have not got far on it."

After his death in 1939, supporters carried on Freud's work. Others rejected some of his ideas and took psychoanalysis in new directions. And in the last quarter century, medication has eclipsed talk therapy altogether as the quickest means to treat mental illness. Nevertheless, thousands of books have been written about Freud; try Googling him and you'll find millions of references. He'd be thrilled.

Not coincidentally, the man who popularized the term "ego" as a scientific concept had a rather large ego himself. He was bound and determined to map *terra incognita*, the unknown, previously inaccessible land of the mind. That was how he'd achieve his biggest dream—to become a famous hero.

And Freud *was* going to be a hero.

CHAPTER ONE

"My Golden Sigi"

ON MAY 6, 1856, young Amalia Freud laid eyes on her firstborn child. Sigismund Schlomo Freud was his name. Later on, he shortened his first name to Sigmund. But to his mama he was and would always be "my golden Sigi."

Clever and obedient, this was obviously a boy who could do no wrong, who would accomplish something brilliant in life. He later acknowledged that he was "his mother's undisputed darling" and always credited his confidence to this. Beautiful, fierce—a "tornado" or a "tyrant," depending on one's point of view—she was almost twenty years younger than her husband, a widower with two grown sons from his earlier marriage.

As much as Amalia idolized Sigi, he soon lost her full attention. Eleven months after his birth, another son, Julius, was born. Like many an older sibling, little Sigi wished his rival out of the way. But then Julius died from an infection before he was a year old. What was the impact on Freud? Looking back on his child-hood, Freud felt he'd been left with a burden of guilt. Had his "wish" come true?

More siblings arrived—six more eventually, all sur-viving childhood—and Sigi was cared for by a beloved nursemaid. When she was caught stealing and sent to prison, Sigi was bereft. All these losses, before he was even three years old.

The Freud home was a shabby one-room apart-ment in Freiberg, a small market town now part of the Czech Republic. Freud's father, Jacob, was a trav-eling wool salesman, a not very successful one, pos-sibly financially irresponsible. The family struggled. Later in life, Freud would appreciate Jacob's "deep wisdom and fantastic lightheartedness," but he felt that his childhood had been clouded by worry.

Still, the extended Freud family was close-knit,

and the children got to frolic in the quiet coun-
tryside, with its soft green meadows and shadowy
forests, the snowy Carpathian mountains in the
background.

Then, in 1859, hoping to make more money, Jacob
uprooted his family. Their eventual new home was
150 miles south—in the big glittering city of Vienna,
Austria, bordered by the beautiful blue Danube River
on one side and forest on the other three. Vienna was
the capital of the huge and powerful Austrian Empire,
stretching from Switzerland to Russia. Like many Jewish
families, the Freuds envisioned a better future for their
children in Vienna, where anti-Semitism—discrimina-
tion against Jews—was on the wane. The emperor,
Franz Joseph, had given Jews some civil rights in 1849.
Full citizenship came in 1867. Now Jews could enter any
profession, own their own homes, and live in any neighborhood, not just the ghetto restricted to them.

But four-year-old Sigi was devastated by the move.
He later claimed to be haunted, even at this tender age,
by the loss of his childhood home, the greatest loss of
all: "I have never got over the longing for my home."
And while he remained in Vienna for almost his entire
life, he continually badmouthed the city—it was

"disgusting." He once wrote, "I hate Vienna with a positively personal hatred." Yet he thrived there—it was to be a zone of comfort he never left, until forced to many years later.

Jacob, on the other hand, failed to thrive in Vienna. For years, the Freuds stayed in a one-room apartment in a dismal, overcrowded neighborhood. This slum was where most Jewish arrivals lived until they could afford to move.

At first, little Sigi was taught by his mother and father at home. At nine he entered a *gymnasium*—a combination of middle and high school. Very academic, very strict. Memorization was the main technique, with a thorough drilling in Greek and Roman classics. Sigi went straight home after school to study all night. He was first in his class almost every year, with perfect marks in all his subjects—languages, religion, physics, math, history, and geography, and even conduct. He could be compassionate and kind. When he was ten, he organized his teachers and other students to make bandages for Austrian soldiers wounded during the war against Prussia (now part of Germany and Poland).

One of Freud's most painful memories was from

age ten. His father, trying to show how times were better for Jews now, recounted an ugly incident he had faced many years before. A man had knocked Jacob's new fur hat off his head into the mud and taunted, "Jew, get off the sidewalk." Sigi was appalled at the racism as well as his father's reaction: Jacob merely picked up his mud-splattered hat and walked away. In this story, his father—supposedly his protec- tor—acted like a coward. This was not the behavior of a hero. If only, the boy thought, Jacob had been more combative, physically confronting his tormentor. Sigi was ashamed.

Vienna's population was the fastest-growing of any European city, exploding to two million by 1910. Businesses were thriving, gorgeous buildings sprang up, parks were landscaped, creative and intellectual endeavors flowered. Along the Ringstrasse, the magi- cal circular boulevard lined with cafés, people nibbled pastries or the famous chocolate dessert, Sacher torte. They sipped wine or coffee and flirted, gossiped, philosophized. Their city had the best doctors and scientists, the best museums and schools, and with- out question the best music. Beethoven, Mozart, Schubert, and Johann Strauss had all lived there. It became the home of composer Gustav Mahler, as well as artist Gustav Klimt and others. Vienna was a mecca for artists. (The young and untalented Adolf Hitler spent seven years there painting—badly.)

Young Freud did love Vienna's museums. But he didn't go to coffeehouses or the fabulous opera house or art galleries. In part this was because he was poor. Also, his passions were quieter. He was one well-read boy, curious about everything in print—German classics, literature from ancient Greece and Rome, contemporary writers and philosophers. He mastered one language after another in school—Latin, Greek, French, perfect English (devouring and memorizing Shakespeare's plays in English), then taught himself Italian and Spanish.

One of his favorite writers was Ludwig Borne, especially an essay of his called "The Art of Becoming an Original Writer in Three Days." Borne advised a writer to take paper and write down "everything that comes into your head" with total honesty and without thinking about it: "You will be quite out of your senses with astonishment at the new and unheard-of thoughts you have had." Automatic writing, this was called.

Freud was a born writer. Like many people, he found his dreams interesting, but he actually took the trouble of writing them down in a notebook every day. No one knew what dreams meant or didn't mean, but to him they were worth putting on paper.

He and his best friend, Eduard Silberstein, exchanged endless letters with poetry and word games, gossip, titles of books they were reading, thoughts about girls.

But he didn't exactly date. "Young ladies are boring," he confided to Eduard. The two teens had formed a secret society they called a "Spanish Academy," speaking Spanish and taking on names of dogs from Cervantes's classic novel, *Don Quixote*. Freud called himself Cipion, a smart, moralistic dog. He felt he had a good grasp on right and wrong. At fifteen, he led a student revolt against a teacher accused of not knowing his material.

Sometimes Freud lectured Eduard on behavior—against tempting a girl into sex before marriage, for example: "A thinking man is his own legislator. . . . But a woman, let alone a girl, has no inherent ethical standard; she can act correctly only if she keeps within the bounds of convention."

As a big brother, Sigi was pompous, even bossy. He helped his younger siblings—a brother and five sisters—with their homework and freely gave advice on how they should behave. He warned one sister against listening to compliments, saying that praise made young girls "vain" and "insufferable." He told another sister that the novels she read were improper for a girl her age.

Disappointed by his weak, unsuccessful father, Freud was dazzled by strong men in history, especially those who combatted their foes. As a little boy, he would reenact battles with his toy soldiers, labeling each with the real names of soldiers. Later he admired military leaders who fought against great odds, like Alexander the Great, who conquered the Persian Empire; Hannibal, the North African general who crossed the Alps to challenge Rome; Oliver Cromwell, a commoner who became ruler of England; and Napoleon, emperor of all Europe. One of Freud's biggest heroes was the Renaissance artist and scientist Leonardo da Vinci—so intellectually curious, so fiercely independent.

He also much admired his mother, who continued to brag about her oldest son. While the rest of the family did without, Freud was allowed to run up debts at the bookstore. His greatest pleasure was in adding one book a month to his personal library.

At sixteen, during his last year at the gymnasium, for his final exam, he translated Sophocles's famous play *Oedipus Rex*, which tells of the Greek hero's tragic end. Oedipus was the fellow in Greek mythology who had become king by answering the riddle of the Sphinx. This monster, half-woman and half-lion, was terrorizing the city of Thebes. The only way to stop her was to solve her riddle: "What walks on four legs in the morning, on two legs at noon, and on three legs in the evening?" Oedipus correctly replied that it was man—who crawls on all fours as a baby, walks upright as an adult, and uses a cane in old age.

So Oedipus vanquished the Sphinx, but during this adventure he ended up killing a man and then marrying his widow. The man turned out to be his father, the woman his own mother. Upon learning what he'd done, Oedipus blinded himself. This tragedy, popular from ancient times to this day, stirred Freud greatly as he put in long hours translating it from Greek into German. Full of significance for him as a student, the story was to reveal even deeper meanings to Freud years later.

Upon graduation, his plan was to go to the University of Vienna and study law. He was ambitious and wanted to help people, just as he'd been improving the lives of his hapless siblings. Perhaps he would become a political leader, now that Jews were allowed to work in the government.

But something else began luring him. When he was seventeen, he attended the World Exhibition in Vienna, a showcase for science and technology, the biggest display thus far in Europe. Freud was so stimulated that he went every day all that summer, seeing thousands of exhibits—steam engines, the latest in first-aid practices, machines that mass-produced goods. The future was in science.

That same year, he went to a public lecture where a scientist read aloud an essay attributed to Germany's great poet, Goethe. Called "On Nature," it was a mushy ode to the mysteries of nature, portrayed as a forever-nurturing mother.

Freud promptly went home and announced in a letter to a friend, "I have determined to become a natural scientist. . . . I shall gain insight into the age-old dossiers of Nature, perhaps even eavesdrop on her eternal processes, and share my findings with anyone who wants to learn."

He was switching from law to science. He made a snap decision that science would be the arena where he would accomplish "deeds of improbable greatness." Freud was never one to underestimate himself. Science would be the weapon he would wield against the forces of darkness, the many problems in the world.

In 1873 he entered the University of Vienna to study zoology, the branch of biology that focuses on animal life.

At this time he had a favorite fantasy. On the university campus were statues of professors from days gone by. He liked to imagine that one day a statue of Sigmund Freud would join them. He could even see the caption on it: a quotation from the play *Oedipus Rex*—"He divined the famous riddle and was a most mighty man."

As he later wrote, a little more modestly, "I felt an overpowering need to understand something of the riddles of the world in which we live and perhaps to contribute something to their solution."

What particular riddle he would solve, he didn't know. Not yet.

CHAPTER TWO

Dissecting Four Hundred Eels

$\mathcal{F}$OR THE NEXT nine years Freud stayed at the University of Vienna, his eye to the microscope.

All the Freuds made sacrifices for Sigi's studies. By now the family lived in a better apartment—but he was the only one with his own room and an oil lamp. The other eight people, crammed into the three bedrooms, had to make do with candlelight. When he complained that a sister's piano practice interfered with his concentration, the piano disappeared. He ate dinner alone in his room, occasionally having friends over for talks about science.

The university was famous for its brilliant science professors, particularly in medicine, most of them trained in Germany. These sterling professors attracted men (women were barred) from all over Europe and even the United States. At the time, students and faculty alike shared a sense of optimism about science, particularly biology. "Biology is truly a land of unlimited possibilities," Freud wrote late in life.

In 1859 Charles Darwin had rocked the world with his book *On the Origin of Species*, containing his theory of evolution by natural selection. His aim was to explain scientifically how the diverse species of plants and animals evolved over time from common ancestors. The constant struggle to exist was a survival of the fittest: Living things born with unusual but useful traits were more likely to find food, ward off prey, and bear young to whom their useful traits would be passed on. Organisms without useful traits were more likely to die before they could reproduce.

Darwin's ideas were reverberating throughout biology and all the sciences—not to mention coffeehouses, parlors, and churches. In university classrooms, the search for physical and chemical forces in nature was on—more natural laws that governed the world of living things.

Darwin's theories were enormously controversial, but Freud was firmly in the camp of those who believed they amounted to "an extraordinary advancement in our understanding of the world." Darwin for Freud was always "the *great* Darwin."

Once at the university, Freud "evolved." He switched from zoology to medicine. He didn't exactly see himself as a traditional doctor tending to patients' physical ailments, although eventually he would have some experience doing this. All Austrian men had to serve in the army, and near the end of his time at college he had to take a year off to nurse sick soldiers. Official reports called him "very considerate and humane" with patients.

But what really motivated him was a general "greed for knowledge." He simply believed that by studying medicine he could learn more.

He took all the required classes for a medical degree and beyond—physiology (the study of the functions of living organisms), physics, botany, chemistry, and every available course in biology. He memorized long passages from medical textbooks. His favorite time was in the laboratory, using a microscope, always careful not to contaminate a specimen with foreign matter of any kind. At first all he wanted in life was "a laboratory and free time."

Later he would change his goal to "a large hospital and plenty of money." From the very beginning, Freud's medical curiosity had unusually lofty aims: He wanted to "restrict some of the evils which befall our bodies."

He was attracted to bacteriology, the new branch of biology dealing with the study of bacteria. Scientists in this field were the first to realize that infectious diseases were caused by small living organisms such as bacteria and other germs. One of the pioneers was German doctor Robert Koch, who was currently trying to isolate the bacteria responsible for tuberculosis. This new germ theory of disease was fascinating—imagine such tiny things, invisible to the naked eye, causing such havoc in the body. Louis Pasteur, the great French biologist, had proven the theory correct, that germs indeed caused disease (and also fermentation). Pasteur was perfecting the process—called pasteurization in his honor—of destroying harmful germs with heat, and was on his way to developing useful vaccines that could actually protect an organism from germs.

Freud admired both Pasteur and Koch, but he was *most* interested in Darwin. And Nicolaus Copernicus, the fifteenth-century Polish astronomer who theorized that the earth was *not* the center of the universe, as everyone thought, but rather the sun. And Johannes Kepler, the German astronomer who built on Copernicus's work and proved that the earth's orbit is oval in shape. Men like these made fundamental changes in the way people saw the world. Freud wanted to be like them, working in a huge arena. Though he was studying medicine, he did not want to heal as much as to be a hero—a scientist-hero, someone who would make a gigantic breakthrough.

Like all of his professors, Freud was a positivist. Positivism was a philosophy that defined real knowledge as only what could be perceived by the senses. People could accumulate such knowledge about themselves and their world, and exercise rational control over both. The dominant trend in Europe during his day, positivism discounted mysticism and spirituality as magic, hocus-pocus, nonsense. The positivist method relied on observation, experimentation, comparison—proof in the form of hard data. Very scientific.

One influential professor was Franz Brentano; Freud took five courses from him. Brentano was a philosopher who called himself an "empirical psychologist"—someone who uses systematic, exact methods in learning about the human mind. Freud also read widely in the works of Ludwig Feuerbach, who moved away from philosophy and theology in favor of anthropology, the science of human development.

His most important mentor was Ernst Brücke, one of the leading scientists of his day. Professor Brücke was a physiologist, one who studies living organisms, including the functioning of their cells and tissues. Freud always referred to him as "the greatest authority I ever met." He worked for five years in Brücke's lab, later saying they were the "happiest years of my youth." Brücke taught that anything in biology could be explained by physical or chemical laws, formulated not from vague ideas, but from painstaking observation and measurements that could be reproduced by others doing the same experiments. In later life Freud always described mental processes with precise words like "drive," "force," "energy"—scientific terms he learned from Brücke.

Freud's first papers had sleep-inducing titles like

"The Posterior Roots in Petromyzon" and "The Nerve Cells of Crayfish." But a burning question of the day was whether the nervous systems of lower animals resembled those of humans. If so, that would be further proof of Darwin's theory of evolution. So researchers in biology were paying lots of attention to simple forms of life. Brücke was working on how the crayfish resembled a human. By assisting him, Freud was helping to prove the theory of evolution in the nervous structures of fish. In the process, he came up with a new method for staining tissue samples with chemicals that would show up the nerve cells.

Freud also studied the structure of eels to learn how they reproduce. Eel reproduction may sound like an early sign of Freud's later fascination with sex. But that was the assignment from his teacher—to test another researcher's claim that he had observed male gonads (sexual organs) in eels. Freud dissected eel after eel after eel—a total of four hundred. Even in the adults, he could find no males. So he theorized that their sex organs came far later in their development. (In the twentieth century, this theory was proved correct.)

He was mastering the scientific method: working

carefully with data (observations), drawing logical conclusions consistent with known facts, and then testing the conclusions. The eel project, with its long hours huddled over a microscope, developed his powers of concentration and observation. Freud was fascinated but torn. He realized that making an actual scientific breakthrough in this labor-intensive fashion could take years. And the pay was notoriously low.

In 1881, after completing the work for his medical degree, he graduated with an M.D. But torn between the need to earn money and the desire to continue research, he kept on learning, living his life of the mind, continuing to live with his parents.

For the next three years, Freud kept a harsh, demanding schedule at the Vienna General Hospital. In what would today be called an internship, he worked under different specialists—surgeons, ophthalmologists, neurologists—gaining experience in different branches of medicine. Almost every department head at the hospital was a celebrity in his field. It had the first-ever dermatology department (formerly called the rash room), where Freud learned about skin diseases. He was a clinical assistant to the influential professor of internal medicine Hermann Nothnagel, who limited his assistants to five hours' sleep a night; Nothnagel approved of Freud and recommended him for promotions.

Even at the prestigious Vienna General Hospital, medicine had far to go. Surgeons often operated by candlelight. British surgeon Joseph Lister had established in 1867 that surgical instruments needed to be sterilized, but it was taking decades for hospitals to implement the practice. Many women at the hospital died during childbirth from a common infection, childbed fever. It was here that Hungarian doctor Ignaz Semmelweis discovered the basic fact that doctors needed to wash their hands to lower the spread of infection. With antibiotics still a long way off, infection was much dreaded.

Freud hated the sight of blood, so continuing on in surgery was not a practical option. He also couldn't stand causing pain. He *was* very much interested in curing serious diseases, especially diseases of childhood. But what most attracted him was neurology, the study of the nervous system.

The word "neurology," meaning "study of the nerves," had been coined in 1664 by Thomas Willis, professor at Oxford University in England. He dissected

corpses in a theater, held the brain up for all his audience to see, and wrote the first textbook on the brain,
detailing its nerves and blood vessels. By 1861 Paul
Broca, a Paris surgeon doing autopsies on stroke vic-
tims, had discovered that speech was controlled by a
particular spot on the left frontal region of the brain.
It was the first anatomical proof that individual parts
of the brain had specific functions. Scientific study of
the brain was an exciting new field.

Freud spent six months training with his mentor,
Theodor Meynert, who hoped to treat diseases of
the mind by finding physical causes in the brain. A
pioneer in brain dissection and research (particularly
the cerebrum and the brainstem), Meynert was in
charge of the hospital's Psychiatric Clinic, the first of
its kind, established especially for him. His book on
psychiatry attempted to classify mental illnesses in
purely anatomical terms.

For ten years Freud worked at a private hospital
for children. He published several papers on childhood
diseases, in particular cerebral palsy, then known as
"infantile cerebral paralysis." He hoped to disprove
the prevalent theory on the cause of the disease—that
a difficult delivery resulted in a lack of oxygen to the

newborn. Instead, he suggested that a difficult delivery was only a sign that the baby had the disease. It was not until the 1980s that Freud's speculations were confirmed, for at least some cases.

Freud gave lectures on brain anatomy to visiting doctors. He dissected brains and researched the medulla oblongata, the part of the brain that controls automatic functions such as the respiratory system and the heart. He was getting more and more interested in how the brain worked. Wouldn't that be heroic—to be the one to unlock its mysteries, solve its riddles?

Not to mention finding out how his own brain worked. In his late teens and twenties, he was developing his own "issues"—periods of anxiety, mood swings, heart palpitations, upset stomach. Neurology could be just the avenue toward understanding himself.

Freud was most interested in the patients at his hospital who were classified as emotionally or mentally ill. He was disturbed at the way they were treated, or rather mistreated—just locked away for years, kept from family and friends. Most doctors didn't dream of listening to their patients, thinking that would only make them more delusional. A good shock was believed helpful—dropping someone into a bathtub of live eels, dripping boiling wax onto someone's palms, a prodding with electric shocks.

Electroshock therapy was the only treatment that seemed to show results, and Freud dutifully learned how to apply it. He consulted the standard textbook, Wilhelm Erb's *Elektrotherapie*. The method helped some patients, which it does even today. But not enough was known about electricity in Freud's day to make electroshock safe; sometimes the patient suffered total memory loss or was severely burned or even killed.

There had to be a better way of helping people already in pain.

CHAPTER THREE

Why Cocaine?

*A*T AGE TWENTY Freud wrote that the beautiful women he saw in Italy were like "specimens" to him: "Since it is not allowed to dissect human beings, I really have nothing to do with them."

Then in 1882, one year out of medical school, he met Martha Bernays, a friend of his sisters'. He caught sight of her peeling an apple in the Freuds' apartment and fell in love on the spot. Gentle, calm, well-educated for a woman of her day, she came from a family of rabbis and well-off intellectuals. He began sending her a rose daily and eventually proposed, even though he had zero funds to set up a household. Martha said yes. But her family's move to northern Germany meant they were apart during their engagement—four long years. They got to know each other not in person, but by exchanging mushy letters—hundreds of them.

In his letters, Freud revealed some very typical nineteenth-century biases. He was going to support Martha, and in return she would obey and take care of him. The end.

He insisted that Martha give up a favorite activity, ice skating, because if she ever lost balance, she might have to lean on another man to stop from falling. He chastised her for "disobedience" when she refused to give up certain customs of her Jewish faith just because he had. Women getting the right to vote? No, politics would only distract them from domestic chores.

And Martha's response? Equally old-fashioned, on the whole. "I want to be the way you want me to be," she wrote back. She didn't show interest in the things that fascinated him, but he didn't expect her to. There is little evidence he ever discussed his work with her.

Freud's notions were more or less in lockstep with those of other middle-class men in Vienna in the nineteenth century. Rigid. It was considered a fact that women were irrational, passive, inferior, pliable. At the University of Vienna, when an anatomy professor argued for women being admitted, the dean responded, "You ought to know perfectly well that women's brains are less developed than those of men." A scholar named Otto Weininger was working on what would become a hugely popular book, about the difference in "cell structure" between the sexes: the male nature was creative and spiritual—the female nature was not. This came cloaked in the guise of scientific "proof" of women's limitations.

Freud never questioned this bias and praised professors for pestering "the beautiful sex so little with scientific knowledge!"

But during his years at the Vienna General Hospital, he was in love, and more motivated than ever to solve some huge riddle—he needed to earn enough money to marry Martha. Still living with his parents, he was so poor that he often couldn't afford train fare to go see her. He economized in every way—once spending what little money he had on a pen with a finer point so he could fit more words on a page.

Part of him would have been content to continue his medical research, but the impoverished life of a researcher would not gain him Martha. "Oh, my little darling, you have but one minor fault; you never win the lottery," he wrote her jokingly.

In his haste to get his shaky career moving, he took a startling turn. His first important published article, in an 1884 medical journal, was on . . . the benefits of using cocaine. Why?

Freud hoped to make a discovery combining his knowledge of the brain as a physical organ with his wish to help people with emotional problems. A chemical, for example, that would act on the brain in a way that would help. Rashly, he convinced himself that cocaine was the scientific breakthrough he'd been looking for. This was a drug that would help people in emotional pain—millions of people, who would then reward him for prescribing this miracle drug.

The drug was then little known, little understood, and still legal. Its habit-forming nature hadn't been discovered. Actually, in the 1880s, drinks containing cocaine were popular—they were called "brain tonics." (The most famous brain tonic of all, Coca-Cola, contained a little cocaine until around 1903.)

Freud read a study in which German doctors had used the drug to increase soldiers' endurance on the battlefield. He ordered his first gram of cocaine from the local apothecary (pharmacy). Using himself as an experimental subject, he swallowed the powder and soon felt great.

Most tellingly, it helped with his own troubling symptoms—anxiety, migraines, and stomach pains. Plus it gave him welcome surges of energy. "In my last serious depression I took cocaine again and a small dose lifted me to the heights in a wonderful fashion," he wrote.

He researched anything he could find for writing "On Coca," his "song of praise to this magical substance." He considered it as an anesthetic, a remedy for morphine addiction, a treatment for stomach problems, a quick fix for seasickness, even a possible cure for diabetes. He gave samples of the drug to his patients, friends, sisters, even Martha. He continued to experiment on himself—for the next several years.

Cocaine *was* found to have a medicinal purpose—but not by Freud. Credit went to Freud's friend and fellow experimenter, Czech eye doctor

Carl Koller. Eye surgery was especially tricky then, requiring that patients stay awake and able to follow instructions, and not bolt in pain. General anesthetics were useless because they put patients to sleep, so the horrific method was to recruit several people to hold a patient down. One day Freud mentioned that cocaine numbed his lips when he drank it. Koller got the idea to try putting it in his patients' eyes before performing surgery.

As a temporary painkiller it worked, but the response varied greatly from one person to another, with side effects sometimes alarming or fatal. For Freud, the outcome of this whole line of research was disastrous. Trying to cure the addiction of a close friend who was using morphine as a painkiller, Freud gave him doses of cocaine. He succeeded only in giving his friend horrible hallucinations and a new addiction. Indeed, some of the early experimenters with cocaine never recovered their health—Freud was lucky in this respect.

As more and more instances of addiction were reported, Freud's marvelous wonder drug started to look suspect. Embarrassed, he dropped the notion of cocaine as a medical miracle. But his reputation was tarnished once the drug was quickly rejected by the medical profession. (In 1914 cocaine was made illegal in the United States except for doctors.) Even today it haunts him—critics who want to call into question Freud's judgment as a scientist will bring up the cocaine episode.

At the very end of his life, Freud would return to the idea that drugs might help patients by correcting chemical imbalances in their brains. Meanwhile, what about an alternative to electroshock, some new, more benign, therapy for treating disturbing behavior?

Following another hunch, Freud left Vienna for Paris in 1885. He was determined to work in the lab of Jean-Martin Charcot, a professor of neurology and then the most famous doctor in France next to Louis Pasteur. Charcot was the resident genius at the Salpêtrière, a huge hospital for several thousand women, many with various symptoms and mysterious illnesses that defied traditional diagnosis.

There was at this time a catch-all diagnosis of "hysteria." It affected patients, almost always women, who were not sick physically, at least as far as doctors could tell, and yet were plagued with mystifying symptoms. The list was long—tics, nausea, coughing, dizziness, severe pains, paralysis, seizures. Some patients seemed depressed, but not all.

The word "hysteria" came from the Greek word for "womb." The ancient Greeks believed that a woman's uterus could wander in the body and inflict these physical symptoms. The cause was physical, not mental. Hippocrates even recommended a serious bout of sneezing to force the uterus to snap back into position.

Later theories had blamed hysterical behavior on demons or satanic possession. Among his patients, Dr. Charcot observed, "there are many who would have been burned in former times"—as witches. He wanted to examine them from the perspective of a physician and find the root cause of the disease.

Charcot and other doctors debated—was hysteria genetic? Was it caused by physical trauma? Were these women faking it? Could a malfunctioning uterus actually be responsible in some way? Or did hysteria originate in the brain? What about lesions (damaged spots) in the brain? In other words, was the disease all in their mind?

One thing was sure—none of the current remedies worked. They ranged from the harmless (a milk diet) to the inhumane (bizarre surgeries). Patients with no money were abandoned in asylums. Those with resources were subject to rest cures. A patient would rest in bed in a dark room for a month (or many months), sometimes sedated with morphine or chloroform, and spoon-fed cold rice pudding and other soft white foods. Shocking the nervous system was thought helpful—hydrotherapy (being sprayed with jets of cold water) or electroshock, including "faradization," or sitting naked with feet in a bucket of water while a doctor used a coil to pass electric current through the body.

Charcot's first attempts to cure hysteria seem equally far-fetched. He devised a special hat for patients to wear that vibrated with an electric motor. He also was known to suspend patients in an iron harness from the ceiling. But his newest method was to treat hysteria through hypnosis.

Hypnosis had been popularized a century earlier by Franz Mesmer, another doctor from Vienna. By staring into patients' eyes and speaking in a slow, soothing voice, Mesmer gradually put patients in a trance. Mesmer would then press the area of the body he believed caused the illness before returning the patient to a conscious state. Mesmer's patients seemed to get better in his care, though other doctors accused him of being a fraud. By Freud's time, Mesmer had been largely discredited, with most medical doctors scorning hypnosis as nothing more than a party trick. Half-asleep, half-awake, patients under hypnosis were not cured, only highly suggestible, apt to do whatever the hypnotist said. But now in the 1880s, Charcot wanted to revive the technique with his patients.

He thought that hypnotism could bring on hysteria in emotionally unstable people. Each week he held a seminar for the public to demonstrate how hypnosis could produce the symptoms of hysteria.

He would hypnotize patients. Once they fell into a trance, he could produce each symptom, one at a time, and then remove them, one by one. Followers of Charcot then went a step further. When they told hypnotized patients that their symptoms would be gone upon awakening, indeed they were.

Something of a performance artist, Charcot drew crowds to his lab. Freud for one was awed. He was learning the power of words, of suggestions, how potent they could be in the context of healing. As he was to write later, "Words were originally magic and to this day words have retained much of their ancient magical power."

Of his nineteen weeks in Paris, Freud wrote, "No other human being has ever affected me in such a way." It was Charcot who introduced Freud to the possibility that physical disorders might have their source in the mind rather than the body.

Alas, Charcot's reputation declined, and eventually his faith in hypnosis was taken no more seriously than Mesmer's. But the seed for Freud's further investigation had been planted.

Freud was galvanized by the idea that hypnotism and hysteria were related in a way *the patient couldn't see.* He had learned in his biology classes all about the germ theory of disease, that organisms unseen by the naked eye could nevertheless wreak havoc within the body. Now he decided that "there could be powerful mental processes which nevertheless remained hidden from the consciousness of men." Charcot's demonstration of hysterical symptoms, such as paralysis of an arm, appearing and disappearing under hypnotic suggestion pointed to the power of purely mental states. Were there forces affecting the mind that the mind was not aware of? If yes, what were they?

Freud's vision of himself as a hero came into sharper focus. He couldn't wait to set up his own practice, so he could learn about this relationship between physical and emotional illness, between the brain as an organ and as a place for "mental processes." He always kept Charcot's photo hanging in his office and saw himself as building on the other doctor's work.

Heady with anticipation, he wrote to Martha, "I will cure all the incurable nervous patients and you will keep me well . . . and they lived happily ever after."

Now thirty years old, he returned to Vienna in February of 1886. He promptly put a notice in the newspaper that a certain Dr. Sigmund Freud was available for consultation on "Nervous Diseases" from one o'clock to two thirty daily.

Eight months later, with some loans from relatives, he finally felt solid enough to marry his true love.

CHAPTER FOUR

The Case of Anna O.

*A*T FIRST FREUD had trouble filling up his few hours of office time.

He kept busy writing letters (more than 20,000 during his life). His letters were filled with details about his children—six of them over the next nine years.

He spent time translating lectures by his idol Charcot and giving unpaid lectures at the University of Vienna. He wrote articles about aphasia, a language disorder resulting from damage to the brain. Carl Wernicke, like him a former student of Meynert's, had just compiled a hefty *Manual of Brain Diseases*, all about aphasia and other brain abnormalities. Freud kept up with his research and attended meetings of Vienna's science societies.

One night he tried to give a lecture to the Society of Physicians. He was excited about his topic—male hysteria, a little-talked-about concept. Several professors in the audience pointed out they had been researching male hysteria for years. Freud felt humiliated and never went back.

But other doctors started referring their difficult patients to him, and he gradually expanded his hours. These were "hysterics" proving impossible to diagnose or cure, mostly educated women with the time and money for treatment.

At this point Freud was using hypnosis. His methods varied, from staring into the eyes of the patient to placing a firm hand on her forehead. He was pleased by how much new personal information, so far concealed, could be retrieved this way. He became more and more intrigued by what he was hearing—abusive parents, grief over the death of a brother, other events that created "powerful mental processes" he was eager to explore. Freud wrote it all down—the women's memories, wishes, fantasies, dreams.

His closest friend at this point was another Viennese doctor, older by fourteen years—Josef Breuer. The two men had the same interests, and the much more experienced Breuer gladly shared all he had learned. Among many other things, Breuer was researching the inner ear's role in keeping one's balance. But most of his time was spent treating wealthy Vienna families, his reputation so high that he was personal doctor to most of the professors at the University of Vienna.

Freud said that talking to Breuer was like "sitting in the sun. . . . He radiates light and warmth." Breuer sent many patients his way and even loaned Freud money during tight times. As a new father—his first child, Mathilde, was born in 1887—Freud needed money more than ever. He wanted to give his children relief from the financial worries that he felt had "robbed" him of his own youth.

The most important patient to Freud at this time was not even his, but one Breuer had treated from 1880 to 1882. "Anna O."

Anna was a true puzzle. (Anna was not her real name—doctors made up names to protect their patients' privacy.) At age twenty-one, she suffered from hysterical symptoms that were wide-ranging and hard to classify. Her arm was paralyzed. She had hearing problems and experienced numbness and headaches. Sometimes she suffered hallucinations about snakes and skeletons, or lost her ability to speak German, her native language, or refused to eat anything except oranges. She had a false pregnancy that gave her labor pains, and she showed evidence of two distinct personalities.

Anna was also highly intelligent and well-read (and frustrated at the limited role for women in her society). She was impressed with a book about catharsis, written, coincidentally, by Martha Freud's uncle Jacob. Catharsis referred to Aristotle's theory of drama, that watching a great tragedy left an audience "purified," feeling safely released from painful emotions like fear and sorrow.

During her treatment with Breuer, it was Anna who noticed that she seemed to get the most relief when she talked about distressing experiences and upsetting fantasies that plagued her. Her symptoms seemed somehow connected to her fantasies. They discovered that if she was able to trace a fantasy (one, for example, involved a fear of snakes) to the original incident that triggered it, then the accompanying symptom would disappear. The process was painstaking, but to Breuer's surprise, it seemed to work.

Anna O. took to calling the method "chimney sweeping," and also came up with the name that is still used, "the talking cure." For Breuer—who got more personally involved with his patients than Freud did—the work was too emotionally draining, and he eventually decided to stop treating hysterics.

But Freud, hearing all about the talking cure secondhand, was thrilled. The case of Anna O. was a crucial factor in Freud's developing theories of mental illness. It was now that he decided that "hysterics suffer mainly from reminiscences." From unpleasant memories, not lesions in the brain or some other physical problem. The painful memories, hidden or repressed, turned into distressing physical symptoms. But the damage from this buildup of energy could be repaired through talk. Talking seemed to relieve the pressure of pent-up emotions that were at the root of the hysterical behavior. Once painful memories could be recalled and understood, the symptoms would disappear or diminish.

Bertha Pappenheim (the real name of the woman

known as Anna O.) was not as completely cured as Breuer claimed. She worsened for a time and had to be hospitalized several times. But eventually she recovered, going on to lead a full life as a social worker; an author of short stories, plays, and books on social issues; and a prominent activist for women's rights. She died in 1936, and in 1954 West Germany issued a postage stamp in her honor.

As Anna O., she is famous for being the first person to undergo psychoanalysis.

This became Freud's new term for the talking cure. Pierre Janet, a doctor doing work similar to Freud's in France, was calling his therapy "psychological analysis." Freud shortened it to "psychoanalysis" to mean his own technique for treating mental illness. His faith in hypnosis had ebbed. He found many patients simply "unhypnotizable." From now on he would use the cathartic method without hypnosis—just listening and questioning.

One of his own patients, "Emmy von N.," was responsible for adding a new dimension to his technique. Since her husband's death, Emmy had experienced tics, stuttering, and hallucinations of rats and snakes. In one of the sessions during her fifteen weeks of treatment, Emmy (real name: Baroness Fanny Moser) made a request. Would Dr. Freud kindly stop interrupting her and just let her talk? Without his questions and comments, she could jump from one thought to another. In this way, she might make connections and better understand the source of her ailments.

This incident prompted Freud to allow patients to freely associate: By expressing any random, seemingly unassociated thoughts that came to mind, the patient could uncover hidden experience. In some ways, free association resembled the automatic writing promoted by Ludwig Börne, the writer Freud had admired in childhood.

Once patients began freely associating, one thought triggered another. The rules of logic no longer applied. Freud encouraged all they said, convinced it would ultimately make sense. Free association appeared to work, although he didn't understand why. Not yet. Each night he feverishly wrote up his observations. Case studies, he was calling them, as though they were police files—and he was the detective, discovering clues.

Freud started to visualize the mind as being like an

iceberg. Most of it was underwater. The part beneath the surface he came to call the unconscious. Freud never claimed to have invented or discovered the unconscious. He always acknowledged the many poets and philosophers before him. He was following a long tradition in literature, from Aristotle and Shakespeare to more recent writers like Samuel Coleridge and William Blake. A few early psychologists—William Wundt in Germany, William James in the United States—had also hypothesized its existence.

But Freud was the first to try to develop a systematic way—a scientific way—to study unconscious mental activity. He poured hours into his case studies—Emmy von N., Lucy R. (a governess haunted by the smell of burned pudding), Katharina (an eighteen-year-old terrified of suffocating), Elisabeth von R. (barely able to walk after her father and sister died). What did these people have in common? What was the pattern? They'd all suffered traumatic experiences—sudden deaths of loved ones, physical or emotional abuse. And they'd all reacted by developing troubling physical symptoms.

According to Freud's understanding, some feelings are simply too painful for people to bear. So they banish the feelings from their conscious mind. The memories remain but are repressed—they go "underwater"—hidden away in the unconscious mind. The painful memories show up as physical symptoms of illness—seizures, paralysis, muteness, and all the other signs of hysteria.

Most scientists of the day believed that when we acquired knowledge and experience, we exercised rational control over them. The brain worked in an orderly, step-by-step fashion. But here was Freud, suggesting that such claims were delusions, that we're not even entirely aware of our own thoughts, and that we often act from wayward unconscious motives.

This was a revolutionary idea, one that turned traditional thinking on its head. Now he was anxious to get his theory out there before anyone else did and received credit. Publishing ideas, sharing discoveries, is an important part of the scientific process. Plus getting himself into print would make his reputation, make him famous. With Breuer, Freud co-authored a book—*Studies in Hysteria*—and published it in 1895. While Breuer wrote about Anna O., Freud presented the other case studies he'd been writing up.

The book failed to rock the world. The medical community mostly ignored it. A few critics pointed out that Freud was blind to certain details that didn't fit in with his theories. Others questioned how his theories could be considered a new science—which is how he always proposed it. Wasn't this a science without experiments and provable results—in other words, a contradiction in terms? And anyway, weren't there simply too many variables in applying science to people's complex minds?

Studies in Hysteria sold only six hundred copies over the next thirteen years. Still, less than ten years into private practice, at age forty, Freud felt he had now earned a place alongside previous scientists who'd shattered their world. Speaking of himself in the third person, he wrote, "Copernicus had displaced humanity from the center of the world; Darwin had compelled it to recognize its kinship with the animals; Freud showed that reason is not master in its own house." In other words, humans behave for reasons of which we're not always aware.

This was very big indeed. A breakthrough. "I have the distinct feeling that I have touched on one of the great secrets of nature," he declared.

CHAPTER FIVE

Nasal Passages

*I*T'S ODD THAT criticism of his first book from other scientists didn't sting Freud more painfully. He was, after all, a medical doctor—he considered his theories scientific. In fact, at the same time as he was writing *Studies in Hysteria* with Breuer, he was also working on a solo effort, a grandiose tome he called "Project for a Scientific Psychology."

By now, of course, psychology was his passion, the study of normal and abnormal behavior. Psychology was still ill-defined, drifting between study of the nervous system—physical symptoms in the body—and the study of behavior. Freud was going to straighten it all out.

"Project for a Scientific Psychology" aimed to offer a blueprint for a whole system, based on what was known about the brain, for describing behavior. The first sentence announced Freud's intention to "furnish a psychology that shall be a natural science." He wanted to prove that his field was another branch of science, with reliable, precise laws similar to Newton's laws of motion and gravity. By what laws does physical energy get converted into mental energy, from one nerve to the next inside the brain?

At first he felt uniquely qualified to accomplish this Herculean task. He'd seen both sides of psychology—in a lab, studying brain cells under a microscope, and in his office, observing the effect of the brain's mysterious workings with real-live patients. How could he describe what he had learned from his office research in terms of a network of cells and fibers? In 1891 a German anatomist, Wilhelm Waldeyer, had named the basic unit of the nervous system—the "neuron." Freud theorized a system of three types of neurons that controlled how energy traveled through the brain.

Knowledge of the makeup of the brain was still

in its infancy, with few shoulders besides Waldeyer's to stand on. Freud quickly reached an impasse. Today we know that neurons in the human brain number 100 billion, and we're *still* researching how they work. But in 1895, so little was known about neurons, much less how they produced mental states, that Freud had to abandon his project as impossibly ambitious. (At least for the time being; parts did reappear in later, influential works.)

He trudged on with his work treating hysterical patients. In some ways so perceptive and ahead of his time, Freud still wandered down strange paths. Just as he had once put faith in cocaine, he put his faith in a fascinating, charismatic biologist from Berlin, Wilhelm Fliess, who had some exceptionally quirky notions of illness. Fliess became Freud's new best friend, and the relationship lasted over ten years.

As a nose and throat doctor, Fliess believed that the nose was the most important organ in the body. It was the cause of all human illness, both physical and psychological. Specific spots in the nasal passages were directly linked to organs in the body. Illness could therefore be cured by . . . nose surgery. Fliess was happy to perform such surgery, or use other techniques, like applying cocaine directly to the nasal membranes.

It sounds cracked, like a Monty Python sketch, almost as if Fliess was putting people on. Yet Freud regarded him as "the new Kepler" who would "unveil the ironclad rules of the biological mechanism to us." Freud also just enjoyed being around his new friend, finding his praise "nectar and ambrosia." He even let Fliess operate on his nose—twice—for distressing symptoms he was having with his heart.

Fliess believed that parts of the nose corresponded to the sexual organs—injuring the nose would affect one's genitals or sex life. Perhaps influenced by Fliess's emphasis on sex, Freud came to identify the root cause of all hysteria. A painful loss or frightening childhood experience? Upsetting, to be sure, but not responsible for hysteria. Oh, no. Repression of sexual urges—that was the key. Because sexuality was so difficult to discuss, patients *didn't* talk about it, and so their repressed feelings morphed into hysterical symptoms.

Why did these two doctors see sex everywhere? One reason was Darwin's influence. Darwin suggested that all biological drives have the same goal—the survival of the species. And the only way a species can survive is through reproduction. All other drives, like hunger, serve the primary one—the sex drive.

In the 1890s polite people never mentioned many parts of the body by name, and certainly kept every inch of themselves covered. Even Martha was once reported to refer to her husband's work as "a form of pornography." With Fliess, Freud could freely discuss his work. Fliess made him feel important, almost heroic.

After quitting his "Project for a Scientific Psychology," Freud busied himself with various other books, the ones later to make him famous. As he wrote, he sent every paragraph to Fliess for comment. During this, his most creative period, Fliess was his biggest influence, his trusted mentor.

Some would say that Freud, in seeking guidance from Fliess, was making a detour from science. The nose?

Fliess's writings were dismissed even in journals of his day as "gobbledygook" and "nothing to do with medicine or natural science." Besides his obsession with noses, he believed in the magical powers of numbers, or numerology. He liked to manipulate the numbers 28 and 23 in various ways, including predicting life spans. Few took this seriously, except Freud. For years he was convinced he was going to die at fifty-one (the combination of 23 plus 28), and he celebrated his fifty-second birthday with great relief.

Fliess wasn't even a competent nose surgeon. Once he operated on one of Freud's patients. He left in a gauze bandage by accident, and the patient suffered terrible complications, almost bleeding to death. Freud was shocked at the botched operation, but he continued to support his friend, and it was several more years before he and Fliess cut off all contact with each other.

Still, it's a condition of geniuses to have an open mind. Fliess may have been a wrong turn, but he was important to Freud, a deliberate broadening of his horizons outside the traditional scientific community. It was to Fliess that he confided in 1900, "I am actually not a man of science at all. . . . I am nothing but a conquistador by temperament—an adventurer." On this question, Freud was forever flip-flopping, unable to decide whether he preferred seeing himself as a respectable man of science or a solitary genius above and beyond traditional science.

In other words, was it possible that even the realm of science was proving too small in his quest to be a hero?

CHAPTER SIX

The Famous Couch

*A*ND EXACTLY WHERE did Freud spend hour after hour listening and observing? In a cluttered office and consulting room next to his apartment. He and his family lived at Berggasse 19, on the floor above a butcher shop, in a respectable neighborhood in the heart of Vienna. Berggasse 19 was to remain the address of his consulting room for almost half a century.

Always the room would be hazy—he smoked as many as twenty cigars a day, claiming they helped focus his mind. The floor was covered with plush Persian carpets, the walls lined with books and sculptures displayed in oak bookcases. Gas lamps gave a soft glow, while a small coal-burning stove provided warmth, as well as moist air from the glass tubes attached to it. No noises came from the street, because the office was in the back of the building. Later he had the room soundproofed. "There was always a feeling of sacred peace and quiet," one patient said.

This was his laboratory, and these were his "experiments"—hour-long visits with hundreds of patients. Through this work he tested and confirmed his theories, achieved new insights, and developed his celebrated technique of psychoanalysis.

He, the analyst, would have the patient (the "analysand") take off his or her shoes and then lie on a couch. The couch, stuffed with horsehair, had lots of comfy pillows on it, and a Persian rug to use as a blanket if needed. Given to him by an appreciative patient, the couch became arguably the most famous one in history. Hanging on the wall above was a painting of Oedipus and the Sphinx, a reference to the famous riddle. Displayed even more prominently was a plaster cast of an idealized Roman woman known as Gradiva.

Freud sat in a large green armchair behind the couch, out of the patient's sight. "Say whatever comes into your mind," he would begin. An hour of listening to the patient talk would pass. Any other noise—a male patient's spare coins falling out of his pants pockets and clattering to the floor, for example—would be jarring.

Before Freud's time, chances for people to talk about their problems were few—perhaps to the clergyman at church or the bartender at the local pub. Even then you would leave out the embarrassing, the outrageous, the frightening feelings you didn't want to admit in public. Here at Berggasse 19 the point was to *not* censor thoughts, wishes, dreams, fantasies. And Freud was neutral—he would not tell a patient what to do, or make judgments, or act in a punishing way. He was on to something new, and he established guidelines as he went along.

Not looking directly at the analyst was supposed to allow patients to relax and feel comfortable revealing their innermost thoughts. They were free to fantasize or say anything at all with no intrusion from the analyst. Mostly Freud spoke just to establish a bond or to reinforce what the patient said.

Partly the seating arrangement was Freud's preference—"I cannot stand being stared at eight hours a day." Partly it was for scientific reasons. In his university training, he learned not to contaminate a specimen

with foreign matter of any kind. A patient was a specimen, the analyst the foreign matter, and he didn't want
to contaminate his data with his own talk. (Some strict
Freudian analysts later interpreted this to mean not
even saying "hello" or "good-bye" to a patient.)

Freud believed psychoanalysis should start with a
trial week, during which he said even less than usual,
so that if he didn't accept the patient it wouldn't
appear as rejection. Patients had to be intelligent, in
a stable period, motivated, younger than fifty (Freud
wasn't sure older people could benefit). Treatment
would last months, even years—five or six hours a
week for a set fee, paid in advance. So the patients
were people with time and money, mostly the wives
and daughters of Vienna's wealthy families.

Observation was the key, a carryover from his days
in the lab studying organisms under a microscope.
Now observation meant listening, but it was more than
that. The initial consultation was always face-to-face.
Anyone who ever met him commented on his X-ray
eyes—once he said, "See, always see, always keep your
eyes open, be aware of everything. . . ."

During the patient's hour he didn't take notes,
and instead concentrated on active listening, gazing
out the window or at items from his precious collec-

tion. Freud's office was as congested as the inside of someone's brain. He adored ancient archeological arti-facts—shelf after shelf of ancient Greek heads, Chinese gods, all-knowing Buddhas, Egyptian death masks, mosaics. He would stare at them, pick them up dur-ing sessions. A friend said his room was more like "an archeologist's study" than a doctor's office. Actually, he often compared himself to an archeologist, digging through the past, excavating layers, helping patients fill in missing pieces of their past. Indeed, one of his heroes was Heinrich Schliemann, whose excavations of ancient Troy and other cities in the 1870s he followed avidly. Freud seldom traveled except to collect more artifacts for his office. He called his first visit to Rome, with its ancient ruins, the "high point of my life."

Ultimately his collection reached 2,000 items (almost rivaling his collection of 2,500 books) and included a bust of himself. His favorite was a bronze statue of Athena, Greek goddess of wisdom.

Freud's collection inspired him—he was able to turn to ancient mythology for insights. He believed uni-versal truths were imbedded in these myths just as he believed that his theories, based primarily on observa-tions of middle-class Viennese, were universally valid. As for his patients, some felt as if these heads of marble or clay were listening to them along with their doctor.

Freud was most interested in helping people suffering from emotional pain. He sincerely wanted to help. "It is essentially a cure through love," he once wrote of psychoanalysis, but not romantic love, which he strove to avoid at all costs. His job was to stay emotionally detached, just as a surgeon "puts aside all his feelings, even his human sympathy, and concentrates his mental forces on the single aim of performing the operation as skillfully as possible." Therapy was like "surgical intervention," and detachment was crucial.

As treatment progressed and he gathered more data, his function changed. He now acted "like a mirror," reflecting the patient's dreams, wishes, but also interpreting, explaining what was *really* being said, what wishes were being repressed, and pointing to the source of those wishes. In this way, he allowed the patients to cure themselves, restoring emotional balance by breaking the cycle of repression.

Freud argued that words were scientific tools: "Words are the essential tool of mental treatment. . . . Nothing takes place in psychoanalysis but an interchange of words."

He wasn't after miracle cures—he hoped to trans-

form "hysterical misery into common unhappiness."
An all-out cure would certainly be welcome, but was
usually out of reach. The goal of therapy was to bring
repressed thoughts and feelings to the conscious level.
Once brought to light, they would lose some of their
crippling power. At this point a patient would be
freed of the symptoms caused by the repressed feelings, and better able to go on with life, to find love
and meaningful work.

Did Freud always follow his own rules? No.
Tending to place too much faith in his abilities, he
once saw a patient for exactly one session and declared
the analysis a success, the patient cured. Occasionally,
patients bored him and he fell asleep.

During the last ten years of his life, his beloved
chow Jofi lay at the foot of the couch and would
get up promptly at the hour to indicate the session
was over. After a patient left, Freud went to his desk
in a study next to the consulting room. Writing up his
notes was step two of his scientific research, and he
took great care with them. He presented his observations in the form of case studies, so detailed and well-
written they read like detective novels.

Freud was no doubt familiar with Arthur Conan

Doyle's literary creation Sherlock Holmes. This master of logic and deduction made his first appearance in 1887, and many have compared Freud's accounts of his patients to these mystery novels. Later in life Freud himself enjoyed a good murder mystery, especially ones by the classic detective-story writers Agatha Christie and Dorothy L. Sayers.

Even if he didn't cure them, patients were usually grateful. For many, it was the first time in their lives that someone had listened to them with full attention. They gained new insights and felt better after treatment—and they told others about it. Some patients were so devoted to their analyst that they went on to become psychoanalysts themselves.

As his reputation spread, Freud was able to charge more, especially once he was promoted from lecturer to full professorship at the University of Vienna. This promotion took several years longer than it should have, partly because anti-Semitism was on the rise once again, partly because he lacked the confidence to go after the promotion aggressively. But he was finally appointed Professor Extraordinarius in 1902. At one point he was supporting his family comfortably with only eight patients.

He saw patients between eight and noon, then wrote up his notes. Martha—besides running a household that included six children, nannies, servants, and her sister Minna—made sure her husband's day ran like clockwork.

Lunch, the main meal of the day, was served precisely at one o'clock. A maid would enter the dining room with a giant soup tureen. Soup was followed by meat, vegetables, and dessert. The doctor liked roast beef with onions, and preferred artichokes to cauliflower. Martha would come to the table with a pitcher of hot water and a napkin so she could immediately blot any spills. Freud usually ate in silence. Sometimes he brought one of his newest artifacts, perhaps a Greek urn with red figures, to the table and contemplated it while munching.

Then he took a walk along the boulevard lined with trees, the fabled Ringstrasse. He'd stop at the barber (he had his mustache and beard trimmed every day), the cigar store, a bookshop, or antique dealers.

He saw more patients between three and nine, ate supper, then played cards with Minna, or walked with Martha or his daughters to a café for ice cream or pastry. Not overtly affectionate, never kissing or cuddling, he was a doting father in his way to his children (all named for friends of his, not his wife's). His letters told about when a baby's first tooth came in, poems they'd written, their accomplishments in school, special talents they had, news about their health. He nursed them when they were ill, which without benefit of modern medicines, was often.

Every Saturday he lectured at the University of Vienna, then played cards with old friends. Every Sunday he had dinner with his adored mother, who still called him "My golden Sigi," and five sisters. In the summers, the Freuds vacationed in the German Alps, and he would take the children on hunts for strawberries or edible mushrooms.

Martha later claimed that during their fifty-three years of marriage, "not one angry word fell between us." She kept a low profile, believing in the popular saying that "The best *Hausfrau* [housewife] is the one about whom the least is said." She did everything for Sigi, laying out his clothes (he always dressed meticulously), even putting the toothpaste on his toothbrush. In matters of religion, she also bowed to her husband's will. Freud, an atheist, banned traditional Jewish customs and ceremonies from his home. (The week after his death, however, she resumed them.) She never interfered with his work and didn't seem to appreciate the newness of what he was doing. He discussed his evolving ideas about therapy more with Minna, her sister. (Some have speculated that Freud and Minna had an affair, but there is no evidence for this.) His marriage was typical of his time; for all his revolutionary ideas, Freud was in many ways a tradition-bound nineteenth-century man.

Freud found that his own bouts of depression vanished during sessions with patients. He admitted sometimes feeling too "weary and apathetic" to talk when he entered the consulting room, but then his spirits would lift. Outside the office, his interests were narrow. He did like to collect jokes and had a large store of them. As for new developments in the arts, he usually disapproved—putting quotes around art when referring to modern "art." He boasted that he was incapable of carrying a tune, and no one who heard him humming Mozart's operas disagreed. The telephone and, later on, the radio, held no interest for him.

Mainly he worked, typically putting in a sixteen-hour day. "I find amusement in nothing else," he admitted.

CHAPTER SEVEN

Dreaming about Dreams

*T*HE DEATH OF his father Jacob in 1897 affected forty-year-old Freud more profoundly that he'd expected. "I now feel quite uprooted," he mourned (even though his mother was still alive). His response was to immerse himself even more in his work, writing several major books, and beginning a bold—and highly questionable—new experiment.

He put himself into psychoanalysis, in the role of both analyst and analysand. It sounds bizarre. But for one thing, there was no other psychoanalyst—Freud was it. And so far, his theories were primarily a result of treating women with hysteria. He felt that, to be universal, the principles of psychoanalysis would also have to include the male mind—a relatively normal one, namely his own. Only in this way could psychoanalysis develop into a complete theory of the mind.

Ever since he had tested cocaine on himself, Freud had always considered his own mind and body suitable for science experiments. Now he spent part of each day on the couch, examining his own childhood and events that had shaped him, analyzing his own dreams and memories. "The chief patient I am preoccupied with is myself" and "my little hysteria," he wrote. Into middle age he was still plagued with depression and irritability, dizzy spells, feelings of worthlessness. He was attempting to take a giant step toward self-understanding.

But Freud himself wondered if he was doing the right thing—his self-analysis was both the first and the last in the history of psychoanalysis. After all, how can one person serve as analyst, remaining detached, while at the same time be the patient remembering highly emotional, often disturbing experiences? It was just too circular to be useful. Too illogical to be considered a part of the scientific process. (All future analysts would undergo analysis with someone

else—who had been analyzed by Freud or someone he had trained.)

Still, Freud felt his own analysis led to certain discoveries. Chief among them was something he called the Oedipus complex. He was convinced, thinking back, that as an infant he had felt an attraction to his young mother and an impulse to get his father out of the way. He interpreted his feelings in terms of the play that had always struck such a deep chord in him—Sophocles' tragedy *Oedipus Rex*. He saw the story as universal: Every little boy desires his mother and wants to remove the one obstacle (his father) that keeps him from his heart's desire. "Removing," according to Freud's Oedipus complex, means an unconscious wish for the father's death. He wasn't suggesting that little boys act out this wish, merely that the wish existed. In normal development, the complex could be mastered by separating from the mother, growing independent, and later finding a suitable replacement: a wife.

Most scientists agree that Freud was now traveling away from science—the study of mental illness—and into different territory—the study of the human condition. In identifying core experiences like the Oedipus complex, he sought a new way of thinking about growing up. His scientific method was starting to resemble storytelling. And as with the unconscious, he was describing things you couldn't see or test. You can't put an Oedipus complex under a microscope—you can't prove it exists. Yet as a core experience it was immediately compelling—a roadmap for every son's journey to adulthood.

What about girls? Freud went on to describe another complex, later named the Electra complex after another figure from Greek mythology. After her father is murdered, Electra avenges his death by slaying her mother and her mother's lover. According to Freud, every girl prefers the affection of her father and subconsciously wants to take her mother's place.

While investigating this complex, Freud's attitudes toward women also steered him into the highly controversial concept of "penis envy," whereby every girl experiences the wish to be male and blames her mother for not giving her a penis. The complex could be resolved only when a girl renounced her desire to be a boy, repressed her attraction to her father, and identified with her mother. Free of feeling inferior, a girl would develop into a healthy woman.

"What does a woman want?" Freud famously asked in later life—and clearly, he was clueless in many ways. In his research, Freud always relied on the male as the "norm" of development. And he accepted the male and female stereotypes of his day. "Anatomy is destiny," Freud insisted in one sweeping statement. What he meant was that gender was the most important factor in shaping a person's life. One of the early female psychoanalysts, Karen Horney, disagreed with him right from the start, the first of many women—and men—to do so.

Another important outcome of his self-analysis was his reliance on dreams as keys to unlocking a person's state of mind. He'd written down his own dreams ever since childhood. Now he studied hundreds of dreams in addition to his own, eagerly seeking descriptions from all his patients, from Martha and his children.

Dream interpretation goes back thousands of years. Dreams were once thought to predict the future or reveal ways to cure the dreamer's illnesses. Educated Europeans of Freud's time believed that dreams were meaningless bits of trivia, a result of indigestion perhaps. Even in "Project for a Scientific Psychology," Freud had called dreams "simply hallucinations motivated by the small residues of energy that are ordinarily left over" from the day and come out during sleep.

But now he became convinced that dreams had an important purpose: to shed light on unconscious desires or wishes. In 1900, he published *The Interpretation of Dreams*, a landmark study of why dreams originate and how they function.

Freud pictured the human mind as an energy system, like a machine. The mind's energy he called "libido"—the biological urge to reproduce, seek stimulation, and achieve goals. This energy would seek whatever outlet it could find. If denied physical expression by the person in everyday waking life, the energy would seek release through dreams, through stories we tell ourselves while sleeping. Wishes sprout like mushrooms in our unconscious sleeping minds. In the language of *The Interpretation of Dreams*, a wish can be satisfied by an imaginary wish fulfillment, or dream. According to Freud, even nightmares are the disguised expression of wish fulfillment. Dreams were a link to the unconscious—in fact, they were "the royal road to a knowledge of the unconscious activities of the mind."

In a dream, he believed, everything is in disguise, every object or event stands for something else. His book provides a guide for the decoding of the symbols, or dreamwork, as Freud called it. In the first paragraph he states: "Every dream reveals itself as a psychical structure which has a meaning and which can be inserted at an assignable point in the mental activities of waking life."

That common dream about being in a public place, among strangers, with no clothes on? We might feel shame and anxiety, but Freud pointed out that the strangers don't seem to notice. "Dreams of being naked are dreams of exhibiting," taking us back to the "unashamed period of childhood. . . . We can regain this Paradise every night in our dreams." We are wishing to be an uninhibited child again.

Or that dream about taking an important exam for which one has not studied? This expresses an uncertainty about passing some sort of test coming up in real life. And that dream about being in danger but unable to move—it means we are stuck between two opposing desires.

Freud saw dreamwork as a valuable code that could help millions of people discover and understand wishes they couldn't face when awake. And interpreting dreams was just "the starting point of a new and deeper science of the mind." In the future, science would explain how normal minds worked, and by extension abnormal minds.

Through dreamwork, valuable long-lost memories from the first few years of life could be retrieved. Freud always advocated more focus on childhood events, believing that the experience of early child-hood related to adult psychology in the same way that the nervous systems of lower animals (like crayfish) showed a connection to the neurology of humans. Children "evolved" into grown-ups. He became a notable contributor to the field of child psychology, the study of children's psychological processes and how they differ from adults'.

Today, even if they reject many of its details, most experts consider *The Interpretation of Dreams* Freud's most important contribution to psychology. He, too, thought it was his most groundbreaking book. "Insight such as this falls to one's lot but once in a lifetime," he said in an instance of being both full of himself and modest at the same time. He was hop-ing his book would have the same instant success as Darwin's *Origin of Species*, almost exactly forty years earlier. Darwin's book had sold out (1,250 copies) its first day of publication. But Freud's took six years to sell 351 copies.

His first lecture on dreams was attended by only three people. "I have not yet seen a trace of anyone who has an inkling of what is significant in it," he complained. He thought of this as his greatest contribution to science. As for the dismal response, he deemed it an utter rejection of golden Sigi. Critics "may abuse my doctrines by day, but I am sure they dream of them by night," he tried to joke about his disappointment.

The next year he published another book now considered a landmark, *The Psychopathology of Everyday Life*. Unconscious desires inform not just our dreams, he announced, but all kinds of everyday acts and behavior. Solving human mysteries, searching for clues, Freud had disciplined himself into a master observer. "He who has eyes to see and ears to hear," he wrote, "becomes convinced that mortals can keep no secret. If their lips are silent, they gossip with their fingertips; betrayal forces its way through every pore."

Secret wishes even show up in mistakes we think we are making accidentally. He popularized the notion of what became called the "Freudian slip"—a seemingly insignificant error, a slip of the tongue or pen, a misreading. Saying "sex" when you meant to say "six," for example. These "errors" are important and purposeful, he explained, because they can be interpreted and tell us about ourselves.

In *Jokes and Their Relation to the Unconscious*, he applied his science to what people find funny. (An unfunny book, it was a scholarly tome complete with footnotes.)

Why do we laugh? Freud asked. Because jokes, like dreams, satisfy deep, unconscious desires. They're a socially acceptable means of expressing the often "unacceptable"—mocking authority, voicing politically incorrect statements, revealing things we're inhibited about, expressing feelings we deem "inappropriate" or may not even consciously be aware of. We think we're using humor purely to be playful or to note the absurdity of life—but really we are giving ourselves away, revealing personal truths in the guise of jokes. "Joke-work," or the analysis of what strikes people as funny, was to Freud a process as serious as dreamwork.

Freud also applied his theories to great artists

like Michelangelo and their works of art. Here he analyzed paintings and sculptures as symbolic expressions of their creators' minds, exploring what dreams and childhood events may have played a part. He devoted a whole book to his hero Leonardo da Vinci, calling him "the first modern natural philosopher," or scientist, for his achievements in other areas besides art. That riddle of Mona Lisa's enigmatic smile? Freud claimed to have solved the mystery, attributing the smile to Caterina, the mother Leonardo barely knew. The artist had lost his mother's smile and was constantly trying to reproduce it.

By 1902, Freud had laid the foundations of Freudianism, his heroic life's work. He was ready for people to support him. For to truly be a hero, a leader, one needs followers.

CHAPTER EIGHT

The Wednesday Psychological Society

S O FAR, IN turn-of-the-century Europe, the medical establishment had been slow to accept Freud. Many referred to him as a "witch doctor" or "the Viennese quack." Critics called psychoanalysis a "scientific fairy tale"; anti-Semitic ones referred to it as a "Jewish swindle."

But *Interpretation of Dreams* hadn't been completely ignored, as Freud claimed. Wilhelm Stekel, a doctor who wrote for a city newspaper, had reviewed it favorably. One day Stekel came to Freud and suggested they form a group to discuss psychoanalysis.

The Wednesday Psychological Society was born

in 1902, a small but cosmopolitan group of Freud's supporters. They were mostly Jewish doctors and other intellectuals from Vienna, plus invited guests from other cities.

Each Wednesday between nine and midnight, future stars of the psychoanalytic movement would gather at Berggasse 19. Early members were Max Kahane, Rudolf Reitler, and Alfred Adler, later joined by others such as Sándor Ferenczi, Carl Gustav Jung, Otto Rank, Ernest Jones, and A.A. Brill. These men were to become the first psychoanalysts after Freud. "So, now you have seen the gang!" he said one night to a guest.

One of them said, "We were like pioneers in a newly discovered land. . . . A spark seemed to jump from one mind to the other." The group was a unique community, questing for the meaning of existence in terms that weren't religious, seeing life as a psychological journey.

The topic of the very first meeting was the psychological urge to smoke—a subject close to the heart of Freud and everyone else in the group. Next to each chair the maid would place an ashtray that was always filled by meeting's end. Freud's children described the atmosphere as "choking" and wondered how the men could even breathe. But in later years, his youngest, Anna, often sat on the stairs nearby, listening, taking in the discussion.

Smoking, munching pastry, and drinking black coffee, the men would mull over case histories, talk about forthcoming publications, analyze public figures or fictional characters. Many also had personal problems of their own they were trying to work out. Meetings became a scientific exhibition of their inner selves—analyzing one another's dreams, revealing embarrassing moments. Nobody dared analyze Freud, once he made it perfectly clear his own problems had already been resolved through his self-analysis. The group would discuss the topic of the night, with Freud making sure he *always* had the last word. He was "hard and relentless in the presentation of his ideas," one said.

This was Freud's personal fan club, a semi-secret society like the Spanish club with Eduard, his best friend from childhood. It had special knowledge, a private language, and stormy relationships. Pleasing Freud was tricky. If you disagreed with him he hated it; if you agreed with him he worried that you might steal his ideas. Admiration was recommended—he was, after all, golden Sigi. But at the same time he didn't really want worship: "I am unsuitable to be a cult object." He settled into the role of benevolent father figure, everyone addressing him as "The Professor." The other men—all younger—competed for Freud's approval and even his patronage—he referred patients to them at his discretion.

Emboldened, perhaps, by his new Wednesday evening support system, in 1905 he published what many consider his most controversial book, all about sex. *Three Essays on the Theory of Sexuality* contained his ideas about sexuality in infant behavior such as thumb-sucking, and in events like toilet-training. Freud worked on the *Sexuality* book at the same time as his *Joke* book, keeping the two manuscripts on tables next to each other.

In explaining children's sexual impulses—still today considered a highly inflammatory subject—Freud was influenced by Darwin's theory of evolution. Darwin demonstrated that human beings did not simply appear on earth in their final form. They were the biological result of many millions of years of change or evolution. Earlier, people (even Freud) had assumed that children had no sexual feelings, and that sexuality simply appeared when a person hit puberty. Freud, however, substituted the idea of an evolving sexuality. He theorized that human sexuality (as well as other aspects of a mature person) had its beginnings in early childhood. From infancy, it grew and evolved. Infants were actually very interesting—Freud saw them as "polymorphously perverse," meaning they got pleasure from any kind of stimulation.

Not everyone agreed—then or now. Some of his first followers parted company with Freud over the very idea of childhood sexuality. But this book was a springboard from which later researchers could refine or oppose his theories. The biggest fans called it a landmark work that freed the twentieth century once and for all from the straightlaced Victorian Age.

If he was looking for fame, he got it. His book on sexuality placed him smack in the limelight. But was he famous or infamous? Now Freud's name was a something of a dirty joke to many respect-able folks in Vienna, one not to be mentioned when ladies were present.

Over the next several years, the atmosphere on Wednesday nights, often testy, grew hostile. The members didn't necessarily think alike. Alfred Adler had some important insights—he introduced the notion of "sibling rivalry" (the idea that brothers and sisters are competitive and jealous), the idea that birth order within a family has a significant effect on personality, and the "inferiority complex" (a feeling of unworthiness that he called a result of bad parenting). But he clashed with Freud in many areas—most notably in his assertion that it wasn't the sex drive but aggression, the desire for power, that was the crucial factor in human development.

Adler up and left the society, taking nine men with him and promptly forming another group. Freud was dead set against the two groups sharing ideas, even though sharing ideas is a fundamental part of the scientific process.

Freud eventually broke—usually bitterly—with virtually all his supporters, for a host of reasons. He could be combative, or sometimes chillingly abrupt. "Dear Sir," he might write to a colleague, "I no longer desire personal contact with you." His rift, particularly brutal, with his former friend, mentor, and earliest collaborator, Josef Breuer, set up a pattern: When, as an old man, Breuer ran into Freud on a Vienna street and opened his arms to give him a warm greeting, Sigi pretended not to see him and walked on.

By 1906 the Wednesday group had seventeen argumentative members. For his fiftieth birthday they pitched in and gave him a medal engraved with Oedipus. Two years later the group moved beyond days of the week and renamed itself the Vienna Psychoanalytic Society. With forty-three men attending, the first international pyschoanalytic conference was held in Salzburg, Austria. The conference high-light was Freud speaking for three hours about "The Rat Man."

This case study was about a twenty-nine-year-old patient mortally afraid of his father or girlfriend being tortured by rats. The only way he was able to get through the day was by performing complicated rituals. (This came to be known as obsessive-compulsive behavior.) Freud attributed the Rat Man's problems in part to his love-hate relationship with his father. This patient, whose real name was Ernst Lanzer, completed his analysis with Freud and went on to live a more or less normal life before dying in World War I.

Freud, as always, was a relaxed, entertaining

speaker, talking without notes. When he stopped, the audience insisted he keep going . . . for another riveting two hours. He often lectured about this case—in fact, more than any other, and listeners were always awed at the skill with which he interpreted his patient's disturbing condition. A witness said he gave "one the feeling of being let out of a dark cellar into broad daylight."

The conference was a hit. It led directly to publication of the first psychoanalytic journal. New Wednesday group-type societies began popping up in Berlin, Zurich, Budapest, and much farther afield—the United States.

Freud's fame was growing—as the head of what was becoming an international movement.

CHAPTER NINE

America Goes Freudian

*A*T PRECISELY ONE P.M. on an early March day of 1907, Carl Jung arrived at Berggasse 19 for lunch. Actually it was a thirteen-hour nonstop talkfest—and typical of his intense relationship with Freud.

Freud, at fifty-one, was looking for an heir. Jung, at thirty-one, seemed to fit the part. A big-time admirer of Freud, Jung was a doctor on the staff of a well-known mental hospital in Switzerland. Jung worked with Eugen Bleuler, a brilliant Swiss psychiatrist famous for labeling a confusing set of symptoms—including delusions and a withdrawal from reality—as schizophrenia (he coined both the terms "schizophrenia" and "autism"). Jung was apply-ing Freudian ideas of talk therapy to patients with this newly discovered mental disorder. Rather than shutting such patients away for life, he and Bleuler believed that they could be treated.

Freud saw in Jung a link to greater credibility in scholarly circles outside psychoanalysis. Jung as well as Bleuler had a solid reputation in the world of traditional medicine, while Freud knew his work was still on the fringes of accepted practice. "It is absolutely essential that I should form ties in the world of general science," he wrote. He also chafed at the prospect of psychoanalysis being labeled an "Austrian-Jewish cult." Jung, neither Jewish nor Austrian, was exactly the man he'd been looking for, my "eldest son . . . my successor . . . crown prince." Here—come stand on my shoulders, Freud seemed to be saying.

The two men kept up their lengthy conversations, and in 1909 traveled together to America, still talk-ing, talking, talking. Clark University in Worcester, Massachusetts, had invited Freud to give the first American lectures on psychoanalysis. Always travel-phobic, he looked for excuses to say no. (Travel frightened him; when leaving on a trip, he would say, "Good-bye—you may never see me again.") At first he said Americans were so prudish about sex that his visit would be pointless, but when the university raised its fee he finally agreed.

As the ship sailed into New York harbor, legend has it that Freud turned to Jung, his young protégé, and said, "If they only knew what we are bringing to them." If the statement is true, Freud wasn't being overly dramatic. America was home to some of the nuttier theories concerning mental illness. At this time, one popular theory held that little nests of germs clustered in the roots of teeth caused insanity. The director of a mental hospital in New Jersey had recently pulled all his own children's teeth as a preventative measure.

Physically and mentally, Freud was now way outside the comfort zone of his orderly life in Vienna. Perhaps that's why he hated America, dismissing the entire country as a "big mistake." It was commercial, vulgar, shallow. The food upset his stomach—especially those crude charcoal-grilled hunks of meat (steaks)—and he was always having trouble finding a bathroom. The people were too informal and lacked respect for his authority, daring to address him as Sigmund!

Even worse, his relationship with Jung deteriorated during the trip. Perhaps a "pretend" son could also harbor an Oedipal death wish toward his "pretend" father. At least that's how Freud interpreted Jung's behavior. The day before they set sail for America, Jung started talking about prehistoric mummies. Freud got so upset that he fainted—he thought Jung was indirectly voicing a desire to be rid of Freud.

On the other hand, as much as Freud complained about the "savage" New World, the United States proved to be a surprisingly fertile field for Freud's seeds.

He made a sterling impression on G. Stanley Hall, a psychologist who had founded the American Psychological Association in 1892 (initial membership: twenty-six). Also on William James, a professor who had set up a psychology lab at Harvard and written *The Principles of Psychology*. He especially impressed James Putnam, a Harvard neurology professor treating hysterics at Massachusetts General

Hospital, who now became convinced that psycho-analysis was the best treatment.

Freud was exhilarated that in "prudish America one could, at least in academic circles, freely discuss and scientifically treat everything that is regarded as improper in everyday life." He felt validated. "Psychoanalysis was no longer a project of delusion, it had become a valuable part of our reality," he said. "It was like the realization of an incredible daydream."

Americans, and not just those in medical circles, were particularly mesmerized by his well-written case studies, with their vivid titles like "The Rat Man" and "The Psychotic Dr. Schreber." Freud's most famous, still-talked-about case was known as "Dora." This was an eighteen-year-old girl whose real name was Ida Bauer. Her symptoms were typical of hysteria—headaches, a constant cough, depression. Her father insisted on treatment after Dora began accusing one of his friends of molesting her. Freud repeatedly dismissed her reports of abuse as an example of repressed desire. "This case has opened smoothly to my collection of picklocks," he boasted. Not that smoothly. Dora angrily broke off treatment after three months. With much more known now about sexual abuse, most therapists today disagree with his handling of her case and believe he should have taken her accusations seriously.

A more successful case study involved "Little Hans," a five-year-old boy with an overpowering fear of horses. To Freud it was a classic example of the Oedipal complex at work, expressing Hans's fear of his father. (Hans's real name was Herbert Graf—he went on to become a stage director of the New York Metropolitan Opera.) In "The Wolf Man," Freud helped a wealthy Russian with depression and obsessions that made it difficult for him to function. Freud traced his patient's problems to a dream, from age four, of seven wolves staring at him menacingly. (Although this man, Sergei Pankejeff, never fully recovered and continued to suffer breakdowns, he took pleasure in answering his phone "Wolf Man here.")

Meanwhile, Freud's old Wednesday group made one final change. In 1910 the group, now the official International Psychoanalytic Association, imposed the first standards and qualifications for analysts—so far anyone analyzed and trained by Freud or one of his followers could advertise himself as one. Freud believed that an analyst should be educated, but not that a medical degree was necessary—doctors were too apt to look at biological causes, not psychological: "I want to protect analysis from the doctors."

In 1911 the first book *on* him appeared. Other psychologists were starting what became known as the Freud industry—in honor of the man who was finally bringing some respectability to psychology. No longer was it viewed as speculation but as a body of knowledge. "My scientific expectations are slowly materializing," he exulted.

The relationship with Jung, however, was beyond repair. Jung had challenged Freud a few too many times. Jung believed, for example, that the mother could be a protective figure, not an object of desire. Childhood trauma was not solely responsible for mental illness. Nor was the libido *the* force driving behavior. Jung hunted for new information, researching different cultures from different periods in history to uncover universal patterns of behavior. (In contrast, Freud looked at other cultures mainly to confirm his existing theories.) Jung saw value to finding evidence that challenged preconceived ideas: "It was a good thing to make occasional incursions into other territories and to look at our subject through a different pair of spectacles."

Freud saw disagreement as betrayal of golden Sigi: "Psychoanalysis is my creation. I consider myself justified in maintaining that. . . . No one can better know than I do what psychoanalysis is." Jung countered that Freud's protégés all became "slavish sons or impudent puppies" because of the way Freud treated them.

Jung was certainly no slavish son. But his research led him to some extreme places—phrenology, UFOs, astrology, alchemy, and many topics that fall under the "New Age" umbrella. Freud himself was interested in the occult. He published three papers on mental telepathy or mind reading (since then totally debunked). For a while he worried his office might be haunted, because of groans coming from two Egyptian grave-markers atop the oak bookcases. Still, he considered himself much more scientific—Jung was dismissed as being positively "mystical." Freud took great pains to defend psychoanalysis from quackery and occultism—"the black tide of mud."

In 1913, after six tumultuous years, his stimulating conversation with his crown prince was over. Jung wrote poetically, quoting *Hamlet*, "The rest is silence." Jung went on to become an extremely influential psychologist in his own right, writing major books, helping the United States during World War II by doing psychoanalytical profiles of Nazi leaders. He died in 1961.

"The truth is for me the absolute aim of science," wrote Freud loftily. Yet as much as he aspired to scientific objectivity, his personal relationships pulled him in the opposite direction. They obscured his ability to see clearly. The more supporters he had, the more possibility of challenge, so the more he closed himself off. He was still open to some new ideas, but mostly if they fit in with his existing theories or came from his own highly original mind.

In the world of science, Freud's continual combativeness could be counterproductive: He had to win. That was more important than listening to new ideas.

"God!" Jung exclaimed years later. "If he had only gotten over himself, it would have been crazy to ever want anything other than to work with him."

CHAPTER TEN

The War Years

*I*N TALKING ABOUT science, Freud was fond of using military terms, even more so than archeological ones. He himself was not opposed to war in general. In fact he thought it cleansed society of corruption and brought out the best in men—loyalty, heroism, dedication.

From 1914 to 1918, Freud saw firsthand what war brought out in men.

On June 28, 1914, the assassination of an Austrian duke by a Serbian revolutionary was the match that lit the fire of World War I. Austria-Hungary—to which Freud was fiercely loyal—declared war on

Serbia, and soon the conflict was global. Russia defended Serbia, while Germany declared war on Russia and then France. England joined the conflict in support of France, and three years later so did the United States. World War I eventually involved more than twenty-five countries.

As for the Great War's effect on Freud and his ideas, the long and terrible years of fighting both hindered and helped.

At first, it all but halted the spread of psycho-analysis as well as its development. Up until now, a relatively stable Europe had allowed for a free flow of ideas. Doctors and patients traveled to other coun-tries to give or receive treatment. Now there were enemy borders. Doctors were to unable to meet for conferences to exchange new ideas or circulate the findings of their research.

Freud remained pro-war. Unlike fellow scien-tist Albert Einstein (and many other scientists), he declined to sign a petition for peace. He was far too old to fight in the army. But he had nothing but pride for his three sons who were in combat.

Then the reports starting coming in of the particu-lar devastation of this "modern" war. Technological advances of the past decades—the telephone, the car, the airplane—had certainly enhanced the quality of life. The nineteenth century saw itself as an age of progress. But "progress" also changed the way war was fought, making it far deadlier. Airplanes dropped bombs, tanks were armed with long-range guns, submarines torpedoed enemy ships, poison gas destroyed soldiers' lungs, and machine guns and artillery made trench warfare shockingly brutal. Death tolls reached staggering numbers. On a single day, five thousand men died within twenty minutes in the trenches of northeast France and Belgium. By the end of the war, Austria-Hungary had lost 1.2 million men.

Every family was affected in some way. Increasingly nervous about his sons, Freud was also concerned about the future of psychoanalysis. "I am living . . . in my private trench," he wrote. He felt more isolated than ever.

During these tense, awful years, he somehow stayed productive, seeing patients and working on his "science of unconscious mental processes." His books became increasingly lofty. He revised his earlier thinking about the divisions of the mind—into conscious and unconscious—as too simplistic.

He proposed a new structure for the mind, dividing it into three parts. In the original German he called them "*es* (it)," "*ich* (I)," and "*überich* (over-I)." In Latin, still the most respectable language in science, they became the Id, Ego, and Superego.

Freud borrowed the term "Id" from the work of German psychoanalyst Georg Groddeck, *The Book of the Id*. An infant is all Id. The Id is not logical, and strives only to gratify primitive needs. It can't distinguish fantasy from reality, thought from deed, moral from immoral. People driven only by Id do whatever is needed to get what they want.

As a healthy child grows older, the Ego develops. Partly conscious and aware of the consequences of behavior, the Ego can apply logic, solve problems, and exercise self-control. Freud liked to compare the Ego to a man on horseback: The horse (Id) is more powerful, but the rider can rein the horse in and lead it down acceptable paths. The more control the rider has, the healthier the person is.

The Superego is last to develop, an internal voice that judges, rewards, and punishes. It represents our conscience and counteracts the selfish Id with ethical rules. "The Id is quite amoral, the Ego tries to be moral, and the Superego can be hyper-moral and cruel," as Freud put it—too judgmental. The three parts of the mind war with one another constantly, in complicated ways, but in a healthy person they operate according to a system of checks and balances.

So the unconscious, according to Freud's latest thinking, was not one homogeneous blob. A healthy Ego adapts to reality and interacts with the outside world in a way that accommodates both Id and Superego. All too often, though, the irrational Id remains in control of people, not the rational Ego.

This was breathtaking—an entire personality theory explaining how healthy minds behave, not just unhealthy ones. Freud boldly proceeded to apply his three-part structure to whole countries.

As the war dragged on and on, naturally his thoughts turned to the psychological basis for war. The conflict knocked over old assumptions about progress and the advancement of civilization—nations were using science and technology *against* each other. Here was hard evidence that the rational mind, even in so-called civilized countries, was not in control. Instead, primitive Id urges, like the instinct to fight and kill, were running amok. Wasn't the war, this ultimate irrational event, proof that his ideas were right? Freud thought so. He wrote, "The world will never again be a happy place. . . . And the saddest thing is that it is exactly the way we should have expected people to behave from our knowledge of psychoanalysis."

The end of the war saw the defeat and collapse of the once-mighty Austro-Hungarian Empire. Besides the 1.2 million casualties, millions more were wounded, or died of starvation or an epidemic of influenza. The victorious Allies wanted to make Germany and Austria pay for starting the war, and to ensure they never became powerful enough to start another. Now a small country, Austria was desperately poor and chaotic. Along with many others, Freud lost his life savings. He grew thin, and was sometimes too cold to work. He needed food more than money, and once asked to be paid for an article in potatoes. He wrote to everyone he knew outside the country, requesting food, clothes, and of course cigars.

But in a strange turn of events, World War I gave psychoanalysis more credibility. All three of Freud's sons had returned from the war without permanent injuries. But many other soldiers were coming back from the unspeakable carnage with a mysterious new ailment. Its symptoms were nightmares, waking flash-backs of being in battle, disabling depression. At first doctors diagnosed the ailment as physical, perhaps the

result of concussions from explosions. "Shell shock," it was labeled. Men suffering from shell shock were often dismissed as weak, in need of more self-control.

But when even officers and soldiers of "good character" started succumbing to shell shock, doctors became desperate to find helpful treatment. At the war's end, 250,000 men around the world were officially diagnosed with "severe mental disability."

In England of 1911, before the war, an entire audience of doctors had stood up and left during a presentation of Freud's ideas. But now British doctors noticed something surprising and revised their earlier contempt for analysis. Like the women discussed in Freud's first book, *Studies on Hysteria*, these soldiers were traumatized. Talk therapy seemed to release the pent-up emotions, relieve the symptoms, allow a man to weave the trauma of battle into his life and move on. Respect for Freudian analysis soared.

To many, the success of psychoanalysis in treating shell shock was solid evidence that unconscious emotions and concealed memories made people sick. Mental illness *was* an illness. Literal shell shock—the physical effect of loud noise or concussion—came to be rejected as a diagnosis. Men were suffering from the psychological effects of war. Twenty years later, by the time America was preparing to enter the second World War, military doctors were required to learn basic psychoanalysis. For the first time the army examined the mental health of its recruits, rejecting almost one out of ten as psychologically unfit for the trauma of war. (Finally, in 1980, after American soldiers who had come back from the Vietnam War showed persistent symptoms similar to shell shock, the syndrome was officially recognized as Post-Traumatic Stress Disorder, or PTSD.)

The casualties of war brought respectability to Freudian theory. By the early 1920s, psychoanalysis institutes had sprouted in London, New York, and Germany. Freud's theories now served to explain cultural, social, artistic, religious, and anthropological trends—leading to changes in sexual attitudes and new developments in the arts. Literature, painting, all forms of creativity were seen to have their roots in the unconscious.

Freud wrote: "I am swimming in satisfaction. . . . My life's work is protected and preserved for the future."

CHAPTER ELEVEN

Becoming a Household Word

*A*FTER THE ONE and only time Sigmund Freud and Albert Einstein met, Freud joked, "He understands as much about psychology as I do about physics, so we had a very pleasant talk." But when friends of Einstein suggested he undergo psychoanalysis, he declined. "I should like very much to remain in the darkness."

Plenty of people—on both sides of the Atlantic—disagreed with Einstein; they preferred to be enlightened. After the war, hundreds of psychoanalysts set up shop in New York. Going beyond serious treatment, psychoanalysis became trendy. "How Freudian" was a common, even chic thing to say.

By the 1920s Freud was a household word. In 1924 he appeared on the cover of *Time* magazine (the first of four times). An American newspaper offered him $25,000 to analyze two notorious murderers. A movie mogul was willing to pay $100,000 if he consulted on a Hollywood love story. Freud declined both offers as tacky publicity stunts that would harm his reputation as a serious scientist. (At the same time, his American nephew, Edward Bernays, was showing corporations how to use advertising to make people want things they didn't need—by appealing to unconscious desires.)

Again and again, Freud refused requests to write articles for popular magazines on subjects like "The Wife's Mental Place in the Home." Psychoanalysis needed to be taken seriously. And yet Freud himself was "evolving" over the years, reconsidering earlier attitudes. His views on women broadened—perhaps because women were some of his most enthusiastic followers. In 1910, he had voted to allow women to join his International Psychoanalytic Association. He gave financial support to Lou Andreas-Salome, one of the first woman psychoanalysts. And he took pride in the fact that his desperately needed "crown prince" turned out to be a princess. In the last year of the Great War, he began psychoanalyzing his own daughter. As she grew up, Anna Freud devoted herself to him, never married, and became a distinguished psychoanalyst in her own right. Considered the founder of the field of child psychoanalysis, she trained noted psychoanalyst Erik Eriksson, who classified the stages of child development still being taught.

Freud could see that his ideas would endure. He had achieved his longtime goals, but his remaining years were bleak.

During the last sixteen years of his life, he lived and worked in a state of pain. In 1923 he was diagnosed with mouth cancer, which doctors attributed directly to his cigar smoking. He had part of his jaw removed in one major operation, with thirty more surgeries to follow. A metal device was inserted in his mouth; he called it the "Monster," and afterward had trouble eating and speaking. Everyone who knew him during this time commented on his heroic courage in the face of perpetual pain. Wanting to keep his mind focused, he refused painkillers, except aspirin toward the end, and he continued to smoke.

When his ninety-five-year-old mother, Amalia, died in 1930, his main reaction was one of relief—she would not be able to watch him die.

His writing became grander, more abstract. He came to view psychoanalysis not purely in terms of individual results (often it wasn't successful, he conceded, or else was required for years and years), but as an investigation into human behavior and society as a whole.

In 1930 he went global, with *Civilization and Its Discontents*. Trying to answer the question "Why are people so unhappy?" his book applied psychoanalysis to the structure of civilization since the beginning of time. It was not a cheery read, but rather an account of how personal drives were incompatible with the demands of society. Irrationality lurks behind the facade of civilization. Whole cultures can grow mentally ill. One way people try to lessen their own unhappiness is by finding some other group they can turn their hatred on. (And he was still lamenting the weaknesses he saw in his father Jacob: "I cannot think of any need in childhood as strong as the need for a father's protection.")

Scholars point out that Freud's bleak perspective

was confirmed by what was going on in the world. World War I was supposed to be "the war to end all wars." It wasn't. Events were leading to the outbreak of World War II, with death and destruction on a level never before seen. Sixty million people were about to die.

In 1933, one-third of Austrians were out of work. Germans suffered as badly. The extreme hardship people endured contributed to the rise in Germany of the Nazi Party and its leader, Adolf Hitler. The main thing would-be artist Hitler had learned during his seven years in Vienna was not how to paint, but how to turn anti-Semitism into an official policy of government. Many Jews, including most psychoanalysts, feared what was coming and started leaving the areas coming under Hitler's control. All of Freud's friends urged him to get out of Vienna—soon. Perhaps to go to America, where glittering notables had honored him on his seventy-fifth birthday at a banquet in New York City. They'd sent him a telegram praising "the intrepid explorer who discovered the submerged continents of the ego and gave a new orientation to science and life."

Ill and old, Freud didn't want to leave Vienna, the comfort of his routine. Several times during his life, even as an elderly man, Freud had physically confronted anti-Semitic harassment, waving his cane, yelling back at tormentors. Unlike his father, he wanted to fight back. Somehow he had the idea that he could take on the Nazis.

The danger got ever closer. Freud's books were burned publicly by the Nazis in Berlin, along with those of Einstein and other Jews, and other psychoanalytical works. "What progress we are making," he mused bitterly. "In the Middle Ages they would have burned me. Now they are content with burning my books." It was a joke, one that he needed to take more seriously.

In 1938, the Nazis took over Austria and immediately began persecution of Jews. The Gestapo, the Nazi political police, kept Berggasse 19 under constant surveillance. At one point police raided the house until an outraged Martha ordered the men to get out. Then Anna was summoned to the local Gestapo headquarters. Though she was later released without harm, Freud was finally frightened enough to leave.

Not without considerable difficulty, he managed to get exit visas for himself and his immediate family. Despite his best efforts, he had to leave four of his sisters behind (the fifth had already moved to New York).

All four later died in Nazi concentration camps.

During his last year and a half, he lived and worked in London. Supporters helped create a near-exact replica of his Berggasse office, including the legendary couch, sent by friends. Famous writers and artists streamed in to visit. By now he was one of the most celebrated men in the world, a tragic hero in exile. British doctors hailed him as the most controversial scientist since Darwin. The scientific Royal Society named him an honorary fellow, whose signature was put alongside Newton's and Einstein's.

He never stopped writing. He began to speculate that psychoanalysts might someday use "particular chemical substances" to help patients, understanding that chemical imbalances in the "mental apparatus," or brain, could be stabilized through medicine. Cocaine had turned out to be a disastrous blind alley, not a medicine after all. But he was correct in predicting a growing emphasis on brain chemistry and the use of medications, prevalent so many years later in treating mental illness.

Freud fought his cancer as long as he could, but finally it began attacking the flesh of his cheek. The smell was so strong that his beloved dog Jofi avoided him.

When the pain became unbearable, he asked his long-time doctor for an overdose of morphine. On September 23, 1939, Sigmund Freud died at age eighty-three.

In one of his last letters, he wrote, "I have spent my whole life standing up for what I have considered to be the scientific truth, even when it was uncomfortable and unpleasant for my fellow man."

His ashes are kept at the Freud Museum in London—in a Greek urn from his own collection.

CHAPTER TWELVE

Freud's Friends and Foes

REUDIAN TENDRILS HAVE crept into all aspects of society.

Throughout the twentieth century, advances in science kept making life more comfortable, more modern, increasingly industrialized. Many people had more education and money, more free time to look inward and think about their place in the world.

Today we take it for granted that there is meaning underneath surface behavior, there sometimes are hidden motives for what we do, physical symptoms of illness can have emotional roots, childhood experiences mold our later life, dreams can have meaning, therapy can be helpful, sex can be openly discussed.

All this is because of Sigmund Freud. Perhaps the most significant contribution Freud made to modern thought was that the unconscious has a coherent structure. Thanks to him, most of us accept that there is a lot of important stuff going on beneath the conscious level.

The practice of psychoanalysis in the United States grew and grew, especially once hundreds of refugee analysts arrived, fleeing Nazi persecution. By the 1950s, psychoanalysis could do no wrong. Talk therapy was seen as an amazing improvement over alternatives like rest cures or electroshock therapy.

New ideas bloomed in relation to—and also in opposition to—Freud's work. The ways people were portrayed in art, books, and movies became more psychologically based. Parents changed the ways they raised children. Freud became part of everyday language—everyone thought they understood the constant references.

Those who treated mental illness climbed aboard Freud's broad shoulders and took psychoanalysis in directions he might or might not have liked. Eventually there were numerous kinds of talk therapy, variations on Freud.

Freud's theories affected all of medicine. Instead

of focusing solely on physical aspects of diseases, doctors began taking into account the relationship between emotions and health.

Then, in the 1970s, Freud's reputation took a tumble. Some of his theories were withstanding the test of time, and some weren't. In particular, American feminists were appalled by what they deemed Freud's debasing attitudes toward women. Most of what he said about women seemed so outdated that it cast doubt on his other ideas.

New technological advances threw some of his theories into question. Dreams as wish fulfillment, for example. By hooking up sleeping patients to machines that show the cycles of sleep, scientists discovered which part of the brain triggers dreaming. It's a primitive area of the brain called the pons, which seems to indicate that dreams are not high priority for the brain, of no great psychological significance. Maybe dreams aren't wish fulfillments, as per Freud, but a way of processing information encountered during the day, or just random recycled scraps with no meaning.

And then there's the scientific method and the trouble it causes for Freudian theories. Where is the hard data to back them up? No brain scan can detect a

Superego; no X-ray can capture a dream; no MRI can translate a Freudian slip. Anecdotal information—what he amassed by analyzing his patients—doesn't count as scientific law. His famous case studies, as perceptive as they may be, are subjective, idiosyncratic. (In one sense, they're an example of how far writing skill can take someone—he was eloquent, convincing, logical. Even when he was wrong.) Much as he tried to remain detached and not "contaminate" the process, his theories were based on *his* perceptions, and his alone, of a tiny segment of humanity. How can they be classified as "universal"—a criterion for any scientific law?

Freud's theories cannot be tested. No one else can repeatedly produce the same results he got. His work is not so much a rigorous system as it is a compelling hypothesis that can be woven around and pertain to just about any situation. He was not systematic enough, but prone to circular thinking. More of a poet, perhaps.

Then there is that problem of not being open to criticism. As Albert Einstein pointed out, "He had a sharp vision; no illusions lulled him to sleep except for an often exaggerated faith in his own ideas." One of the requirements of a scientist is considering evidence that points to the truth of other theories or the flaws in one's own—not one of Freud's strengths.

The harshest critics see his work as mumbo jumbo, pseudoscience, a joke. "Freud was as nutty as could be," said the founder of a rival form of talk therapy. In 2004 a newspaper editorialized, "Arguably no other notable figure in history was so fantastically wrong about nearly every important thing he had to say."

Headlines show the ongoing duel over his work: "Is Freud Dead?" (1993) versus "Why Freud Isn't Dead" (1996) versus "What Freud Got Right" (2002). Many psychiatrists today would agree that some aspects of Freudian psychoanalysis may be useful, but only as one of many treatments.

As Freud himself predicted, by the mid-twentieth century, scientists discovered drugs that could provide dramatic help for mental illness by adjusting the brain's chemistry. Thorazine for schizophrenia went on the market in the United States in 1954, then lithium for manic depression, now referred to as bipolar disorder. In the 1980s, antidepressants such as Prozac were first prescribed for people with less severe illnesses. Brain-altering chemicals are today a multi-billion dollar business. Doctors and patients value them as a less expensive, less time-consuming, and often more effective treatment than talk therapy.

Take obsessive-compulsive disorder. A symptom might be constant hand-washing because of an overpowering fear of germs. Freud thought that meant a patient was fixated in the anal stage of infancy. The cause, however, as many scientists now believe, may lie with unbalanced biochemicals in a part of the brain called the caudate nucleus. Rather than spending hours on a couch, a patient may simply take a medication to correct the imbalance.

Freud did unlock doors for others, open up channels for thought, pave the way for modern psychology—even neurochemistry. Medical doctors and neuroscientists all see further—and have a much different view of emotional terrain—because of standing on his shoulders.

Many questions he tried to answer *still* go unanswered. How much is still left to understand about the physical brain versus the invisible mind? New insights and treatments for mental illness are certain to come from the study of genetics, the field of brain imaging, and yet-to-be-discovered technologies. A new journal has been established that combines Freud with contemporary neuroscience, claiming that the more scientists learn about the physical structure of the brain, the more support there is for some of his theories.

Meanwhile, the diagnosis of hysteria—initially the

basis for Freud's career—quietly went away. As psychiatrists learned more, they realized the label was way too
broad. A wide range of specific mental illnesses and disorders (hysteria was excluded) were categorized in 1952.
The American Psychiatric Association published *The
Diagnostic and Statistical Manual of Mental Disorders*
(DSM), and revises it every few years.

But Freud himself never goes away—a flawed but
stubborn visionary. As the poet W. H. Auden wrote,
"to us he is no more a person/now but a whole
climate of opinion." Psychoanalysis continues to be
practiced. His theories of childhood development are
still taught in universities. In 1999 he was named one
of *Time* magazine's 100 Most Important People of
the Century. Any tome about human behavior will
include endless references to Freud. He is responsible
for how we understand ourselves.

You can see an exact replica of the famous couch
and his office at the Freud Museum in London. If jokes
are a barometer, you can laugh at more jokes about
Freud than about any other scientist. And if you want,
you can even buy a pair of cozy shoes with fuzzy Sigi
heads on them. They're called Freudian slippers.

APPENDIX

Major Works by Sigmund Freud

Studies on Hysteria, 1895

The Interpretation of Dreams, 1900

The Psychopathology of Everyday Life, 1901

Three Essays on the Theory of Sexuality, 1905

Jokes and Their Relation to the Unconscious, 1905

Five Lectures on Psychoanalysis, 1910

Totem and Taboo: Resemblances Between the Psychic Lives of Savages and Neurotics, 1913

On the History of the Psychoanalytic Movement, 1914

Introductory Lectures on Psychoanalysis, 1917

Beyond the Pleasure Principle, 1920

The Ego and the Id, 1923

Inhibitions, Symptoms, and Anxiety, 1926

The Question of Lay-Analyses, 1926

The Future of an Illusion, 1927

Civilization and Its Discontents, 1930

New Introductory Lectures on Psycho-Analysis, 1933

Moses and Monotheism, 1939

BIBLIOGRAPHY

(* books especially for young readers)

Adler, Robert E. *Medical Firsts: From Hippocrates to the Human Genome.* New York: Wiley, 2004.

Breger, Louis. *Freud: Darkness in the Midst of Vision.* New York: Wiley, 2000.

Cole, Michael, with **Sheila Cole** and **Cynthia Lightfoot.** *The Development of Children.* New York: Worth Publishers, fifth edition, 2004.

Ellenberger, Henri F. *The Discovery of the Unconscious: The History and Evolution of Dynamic Psychiatry.* New York: Basic Books, 1970.

Flam, Lydia. *Freud the Man: An Intellectual Biography.* New York: Other Press, 2003.

Gadwall, Lynn. *Madness in America: Cultural and Medical Perceptions of Mental Illness Before 1914.* Ithaca, New York: Cornell University Press, 1995.

Gay, Peter. *Freud: A Life for Our Time.* New York: Norton, 1998.

Heller, Sharon. *Freud A to Z.* New York: Wiley, 2005.

* Inquest, H. P. *The Great Brain Book: An Inside Look at the Inside of Your Head.* New York: Scholastic, 2004.

Johnston, William M. *Vienna, Vienna: The Golden Age, 1815–1914.* New York: Crown, 1980.

* **Muckenhoupt, Margaret.** *Sigmund Freud, Explorer of the Unconscious.* New York: Oxford University Press, 1997.

Panek, Richard. *The Invisible Century: Einstein, Freud, and the Search for Hidden Universes.* New York: Viking, 2004.

Porter, Roy. *Madness: A Brief History.* New York: Oxford University Press, 2002.

Porter, Roy. *A Social History of Madness: The World Through the Eyes of the Insane.* New York: Dutton, 1987.

* **Reef, Catherine.** *Sigmund Freud: Pioneer of the Mind.* New York: Clarion, 2001.

Robinson, Paul A. *Freud and His Critics.* Berkeley, CA: University of California Press, 1993.

Webster, Richard. *Why Freud Was Wrong: Sin, Science, and Psychoanalysis.* New York: HarperCollins, 1995.

Zaretsky, Eli. *Secrets of the Soul: A Social and Cultural History of Psychoanalysis.* New York: Knopf, 2004.

Zimmer, Carl. *Soul Made Flesh: The Discovery of the Brain—and How It Changed the World.* New York: The Free Press, 2004.

WEB SITES
(Verified May 2006)

The American Psychiatric Association: http://www.psych.org/

The American Psychoanalytic Association: http://www.apsa.org/index.htm

Freud Museum, London: http://www.freud.org.uk/

Sigmund Freud Museum, Vienna: http://www.freud-museum.at/e/index.html (includes a video library)

"Sigmund Freud: Conflict and Culture": http://www.loc.gov/exhibits/freud/ (includes home movie footage of Freud between 1929 and 1937)

National Institute of Mental Health: http://www.nimh.nih.gov/

"Neuroscience for Kids": http://faculty.washington.edu/chudler/neurok.html

The New York Psychoanalytic Society and Institute: http://www.psychoanalysis.org/index.html

Young Dr. Freud, PBS special: http://www.pbs.org/youngdrfreud/

INDEX